Cycling Cultures

Cycling Cultures

edited by Peter Cox

University of Chester Press

First published 2015
by University of Chester Press
University of Chester
Parkgate Road
Chester CH1 4BJ

Printed and bound in the UK by the
LIS Print Unit
University of Chester
Cover designed by the
LIS Graphics Team
University of Chester

A catalogue record for this book is available from the British
Library

ISBN 978-1-908258-11-3

CONTENTS

List of Figures   vii

List of Tables   viii

Acknowledgements   ix

Notes on Contributors   x

Foreword   xiii

Introduction: Why Cycling Cultures?   1
Peter Cox

Chapter 1
Cycling Cultures and Social Theory   14
Peter Cox

Chapter 2
Diversity in Cycle Policies   43
Ida H. J. Sabelis

Chapter 3
Rhetoric and Reality: Understanding the   63
English Cycling Situation
Dave Horton and Tim Jones

Chapter 4
Lessons Learned Through Training Immigrant   78
Women in the Netherlands to Cycle
Angela van der Kloof

Chapter 5
Mapping Everyday Cycling in London   106
Brian Deegan

Chapter 6
Cargo Bikes: Distributing Consumer Goods   130
Peter Cox and Randy Rzewnicki

Chapter 7
Randonneurship – a Modern Cycling Construction   152
Heike Bunte

Chapter 8
Women, Gendered Roles, Domesticity and Cycling in   174
Britain, 1930–1980
Peter Cox

Postscript: Cycling Cultures, Culture and Cycling   203
Peter Cox

LIST OF FIGURES

Figure 1.1. Three-dimensional grid mapping of the relationship between different types of bicycle.   19

Figure 1.2. Attitudes to the bicycle and the ride.   23

Figure 2.1. Population density for Provinces in the Netherlands and their political party logos. *Source: Hans van Nieuwstraten.*   50

Figure 2.2. Incidence of reference to fiets (bicycle) in political manifestoes, by party and Province.   59

Figure 4.1. Maslow's four stages of learning.   89

Figure 4.2. A person's motility in relation to tacit knowledge and the environment.   94

LIST OF TABLES

Table 2.1. Incidence of references to fiets (bicycle) in   51
political manifestoes, by party and Province.
Source: Hans van Nieuwstraten.

Table 2.2. Score sheet for cycle friendliness in the   52
political programmes in relation to commuting by
long distances or everyday, shorter distance cycling.
Source: Hans van Nieuwstraten.

Table 4.1. Bicycle travel time per person, per day   81
according to age, gender and region (in minutes).

Table 4.2. Number of bicycle trips per person, per day   82
according to age and gender.

Table 4.3. Bicycle travel time per person, per day   83
according to gender and education (in minutes).

Table 4.4. Number of bicycle trips per person, per day   83
according to gender and education.

Table 4.5. Bicycle travel time per person, per day   86
according to gender, country of birth and level of
urbanization (in minutes).

ACKNOWLEDGEMENTS

Thanks go to the Leverhulme Trust whose International Academic Fellowship funding (2014–15) provided me the opportunity to work specifically on "Developing Cross-Disciplinary Research into Bicycling and the Environment" at the Rachel Carson Center for Environment and Society (RCC). The RCC, a joint project of the LMU (Ludwig Maximilian University) and Deutsches Museum, Munich provided the opportunity to hone the ideas here, finish the writing and gave me a much deeper insight into the interdisciplinary perspectives they have pioneered. Acknowledgement must also be made to undergraduate students of the University of Chester over a number of years on taught modules in both Popular Culture (SO6703) and in Social Change and Social Movements (SO6102). Their discussions and contributions have been integral to the shaping of my understanding of the ideas in Chapter One. Thanks also to Sarah Griffiths at the University of Chester Press whose skills and patience have made working on the book such a good experience, and to the contributors for making it incredibly stress free.

NOTES ON CONTRIBUTORS

Heike Bunte worked as a trained cycle mechanic for over ten years before finishing her MA in Economic and Sociological Studies in 2009. Her main studies and empirical research are on the sociology of cycling, sport and the body, corporate mobility management, spatial mobility and the mobility behaviour of aged woman in big cities. After working for the Technical University in Dresden on an empirical research program with 300 elderly people on cycling and safety, she currently works on national cycling issues for The Federal Environment Agency in Dessau-Roßlau.

Peter Cox began working on the sociology of cycling in 2004 after working in the bicycle trade and as an environmental activist. With Dave Horton and Paul Rosen he was a Co-Editor of *Cycling and Society* (Ashgate Publishing, 2007). He teaches in the Department of Social and Political Science at the University of Chester and in 2014–15 was a Leverhulme International Academic Fellow, working at the Rachel Carson Center for Environment and Society in Munich. His interdisciplinary research combines both historical archive work and ethnographic methods to investigate cycling practices.

Brian Deegan is a Principal Technical Specialist in cycling at Transport for London. He was one of the main authors of the London Cycling Design Standards (2014) and is a UK pioneer of protected cycle lanes. He has written several published technical articles covering cycle planning and engineering including; "Raising the Bar" (2014) and "Thematic Report into Commuter Travel Patterns" (2010) for the European Transport Safety Council, "Cities for Cycling" (2013) for CIVITAS, "The Science of Cycle Networks" (2012) for Landor Publications and "Planning Networks for Cycling: Relevant Human Factors and Design Processes" (2010) for the *Proceedings of the Institute of Civil*

Engineering – Engineering Sustainability journal. He is one of the UK's leading experts in cycle route design and is currently working on delivering the Mayor of London's £913 million *Vision for Cycling*. He is a member of the Scientists for Cycling group and the Cycling and Society Research Group and affiliated with several professional institutions.

Dave Horton is a sociologist and cycling enthusiast based in Lancaster in north-west England. He is a founder member of the Cycling & Society Research Group, and Co-Editor of *Cycling and Society* (Ashgate Publishing, 2007). Along with Tim Jones, between 2008 and 2011 he worked on a research project, *Understanding Walking and Cycling*, that explored the state of, and prospects for, walking and cycling in England. Dave is active in local cycling cultures, and blogs at: thinkingaboutcycling.com.

Tim Jones is a Senior Research Fellow within the Faculty of Technology, Design and the Environment at Oxford Brookes University. He is currently Principal Investigator on the UK *cycle BOOM (Design for Lifelong Health & Wellbeing)* study which is investigating cycling and older age and was previously Co-Investigator on the UK *Understanding Walking and Cycling* study. Tim is interested in studying the practice of walking and cycling through a sociological and geographical lens and using novel multi-method approaches to understanding urban mobility and the implications for planning and design.

Angela van der Kloof is an enthusiastic consultant at Mobycon, an independent consultancy in mobility, traffic and transport solutions. She enjoys challenging people to think differently, as she learned to do more than twenty years ago when she began teaching immigrant women to cycle. She initiated and developed a series of train-the-trainers sessions and took the lead in the production of an instruction video and booklets for cycling teachers in the Netherlands. Understanding the fundamental way in which mobility affected the lives of the women she was teaching, Angela began to see the bike as a tool to stimulate participation and interaction in society and create an environment that is social and accessible for all. She shares her experience, knowledge and enthusiasm in training, articles, presentations, workshops and on social media.

Randy Rzewnicki Following his PhD in Kinesiology at KU Leuven, Belgium, in 2003, Randy Rzewnicki has worked for cycling campaigners at the local, national and European level. At the European Cyclists' Federation (ECF) since 2008, he has managed a number of EU funded projects including Cyclelogistics and Pro-E-Bike which promoted moving goods by cycle. Married with three children, and no car, he and his spouse both regularly use their Bakfiets cargo bike in Brussels.

Ida Sabelis is Associate Professor at the Department of Organisational Sciences, Faculty of Social Sciences at VU University in Amsterdam. Her specialism is diversity in organizations (culture, class, gender, age, etc.) coupled with cultural (mis)understanding of time and temporality. The latter theme triggered an interest in futures, sustainability, and transdisciplinary studies on "post fossil", or "active mobility", also via the Zeitakademie Group in Tutzing, Germany. She is a cycle activist, commuting with a Velomobile between her home town and Amsterdam, and former board member of the NVHPV (the Dutch Association of Human Powered Vehicles). She is Editor-in-Chief of the international journal *Gender, Work and Organization*, board member of *Time & Society* and member of Scientists for Cycling from the ECF.

FOREWORD

As President of the European Cyclists' Federation (ECF) and the World Cycling Alliance (WCA), I am delighted to welcome the publication of *Cycling Cultures*. I am sure this is the right time for this book and the right time for this debate about what we mean by cycling cultures. Over the past few years we have laid the foundations for this discussion in ECF's Scientists for Cycling network with the support of Peter Cox, Editor and friend, and all his colleagues and authors in this publication, so it is right that their work comes forward as a complete volume to encourage further discussions.

For me, the discussion about cycling cultures is all about the contradictions we face in trying to show the role of cycling in a sustainable, person-centred world. Cycling has regional roots and has developed different roles due to diverse human histories, but now we want to see it as a global issue in light of the global exchange of products and mobility development. Coming from planning traditions, transport technologies have been in the forefront of so-called "modernization", but this dominance has pushed human needs and basic rights to become a lower priority.

This brings us to the first question. Do we have – as often heard – cycling cultures? And, if we do, how can we understand and value their diversity while taking a global approach? Cultural uniqueness and diversity are important in times where technologies have taken the lead, but what about the adaptation of societies and their individual members to the outlines of their own histories, their climate and environment, their societal specifics and their great ideas of their own future?

We expect cultures to be diverse and quite pluralistic. What a good message, for it means nobody can conquer the world with a simple blueprint. As cultural practices meet, sometimes we see a fruitful merger, sometimes less so. We have always had "old meets new" but something is different now. Cultural exchange is a global phenomenon, and we face the troubles and have responsibility for these developments. So my second question is whether cycling can avoid these risks and be a source of cultural exchange that strengthens society? I hope this book is a valuable resource for answering these questions.

I may have questions about cycling culture, but I also have confidence in the cycling community that is bringing insight to the topic. Scientists for Cycling is the ECF global network that has been setting the agenda for cycling policy since the Velo-city 2010 conference in Copenhagen. Since the formal launch of the network, the topic of culture has increased in priority in our discussions and featured in our events, due to the work of authors here, alongside other colleagues. Velo-city 2013 in Vienna even adopted the conference subtitle: "The Sound of Cycling – Urban Cycling Cultures".

With this leadership, cycling cultures has become one of nine key issues in the Scientists for Cycling agenda for cycling research. Here we opened a new chapter with the methodological approach of "framing" these key issues of our agenda. This has also meant changing academic and policy cultures, because we have had to re-set cycling from its perception as a narrow, defensive niche activity to begin to occupy the mainstream of transport policy. As an interesting experience we realized that contributions collected in this way were even widening the frame, discovering and reflecting cycling potentials for policy, research and societies.

The book covers an important subject, with high quality contributors, at just the right time in our cycling agenda setting. The examples are numerous, their importance valuable and the questions far-reaching. I particularly appreciate that the variety of chapters means we can look at the discussions in the widest possible way. For example, cargo cycling is not considered only about carrying goods from A to B as a tool for business and private use, it is changing the whole scenario of integrated transport and the rhythm of daily life – for people and their societies.

We as the ECF and the advocacy community must play our part. For the ECF and its global structure, the WCA, it is not enough to be the professional facilitator of all cycling-related issues. Through the Velo-city conference series and our global networks we must also have the mission to stimulate the pluralism and diversity of cycling cultures for a sustainable mobility all over the world.

Thank you to my colleagues in the Scientists for Cycling network for your important role stimulating this from the academic point of view and of course my thanks again to all contributors for this cycling cultures book, the diversities described and the richness of cycling outlined for all people. Cycling cultures are on stage.

Manfred Neun
President of the ECF and WCA
Chair of the Scientists for Cycling Advisory Board

INTRODUCTION

WHY CYCLING CULTURES?

Peter Cox

Travelling through numerous European cities, one cannot but be struck by the proliferation of bicycles, whether parked on the streets or in transit; on roads, cycleways and other paths. Closer inspection may alert the tourist to a diversity in styles and designs of bicycles used today, and to the tremendous diversity of their riders. This book is both a reflection of the renewed popular interest in cycling, in many different forms, and an academic consideration of what that profusion of perspectives might mean.

The first idea for this book on cycling cultures was to present a series of case studies in a straightforward way that would illustrate some of this diversity. But which cases to choose? Which examples and why? What selection would be appropriate to demonstrate the variety of practices concealed within the bland singularity of the term "cycling"? Should it aspire to being somehow representative – if that were indeed possible – or should it deliberately specialize in a particular group of studies? As thinking and planning progressed, it became clear that case studies alone would not help in understanding what this diversity means – for the implications and significance of the diversity of activity subsumed under the singular title of "cycling" is not just an abstract or academic question for the study of different social forms. It also belies a pressing policy question.

If a nation, a region or a city is to have a cycling policy, what might this actually mean in light of cultural diversity? What are the pressures that it needs to deal with and how might it approach them? How can a single policy be made inclusive if it

1

covers such diversity: what assumptions are (to be) made in such policies about the bicycle user(s)?

Therefore, a second approach began to take shape. Rather than trying to be comprehensive or representative, the chapters instead reflect a series of conversations taking place at the bridging point of academia, activism and public policy. While individual chapters can be taken as studies on their own, they also seek to inform a more central set of shared concerns with questions of diversity and complexity in cycling practices and experiences. The authors have a mixture of academic and professional backgrounds and the analyses presented here are strongly indebted to the fluid and porous boundaries between these worlds. What brings them together is not just an interest in the general topic, but the shared conversations that these texts represent, as the writers attempt to grapple with both the reality of the diversity of cycling cultures and their implications for policy and practice. Between them, they have all been concerned with questions of cycling practices, asking how that practice is constructed and what it means in different contexts to different audiences. In the work here, cycling is not just as a physical practice but a tremendously differentiated series of sites of cultural practices. These conversations take place across the differing social and political contexts, mainly of the UK and the Netherlands but also with perspectives from Germany and Belgium, revealing both contrasts and continuities, despite very different levels of activity, policy and investment. Discussions have taken place under the auspices of a number of networks, particularly the Cycling and Society Research Group (CSRG) and the European Cyclists' Federation (ECF) supported Velo-city conferences. From a range of perspectives and interests, the chapters here share a common interest in understanding and exploring diversity in connection with cycling. From their different viewpoints, they seek to unpack the singularity of the terms "cycling" and "cyclist" to reveal the ways in which these figures are constructed from complex and interwoven strands. The studies reveal changing images over time and differing geographical experiences alongside styles and subcultures that have the capacity to cross borders. The book's intention is to provide the reader with a glimpse not simply of the breadth of actors and activities concealed within the linguistic singularity of "cycling", but to provide ways of making sense of those diverse characteristics. Its structure reflects a shared desire by the authors not simply to present a series of discrete chapters, but to demonstrate how a range of voices and widely different topics can inform a shared concern with issues of diversity. The editorial voice among these is, although sole authored, a product of these conversations.

As the chapters show, the variety of cycling activities and the diversity of practices spring from profoundly differing experiences, personal and collective, shaped by national histories, class, gender and ethnicity. We should additionally note that bicycle uses, and the ways of thinking about riding, which can only be very briefly mentioned here, are profoundly different as contexts change. They range from mundane riding as transport just to get oneself or cargo around, through to riding purely for the joy and challenge in various leisure forms, however, organized or unorganized. Competitive sport, especially at amateur level is also cycling and such riders need to fall within the remit of policy provision covering use of public space, especially as their activity requires hours of dedicated training beyond the short moments of competitive activity.

Thus we also have a variety of terrains to consider – roads, paths and those off-road routes that fall under neither broad description. What regulations should be in place to govern these activities? How should machinery be regulated – even perhaps, should the same regulations apply to all cycles: are the build and design standards for a cargo bike designed to carry 100 kg loads still appropriate to a 7 kg racing machine? ISO standards recognize the need for different regulations for specialist designs; to what extent might other legal regulations need to think about this diversity? By exploding simplistic reductionism, these chapters can, perhaps, make a modest contribution to the debates over planning for cycling as well as being a study in the application of social theory to explicate real life situations.

As an academic text, this volume can first be located within the social science literature on mobilities appearing in the past ten years. Second, it is part of a relatively new range of academic studies on cycling from perspectives within the social sciences and humanities. Urry (2008, p. 14) maps, "five interdependent 'mobilities' that produce social life organised across distance". These are summarized as "the corporeal travel of people"; "the physical movement of objects to producers, consumers and retailers"; "the imaginative travel effected through the images of places and peoples"; "virtual travel, often in real time", and "the communicative travel through person to person messages". Across these different mobilities, we see the case studies in this volume reflecting this production of social life; whether in the imaginative travel produced by mapping and by associated guidebooks (Deegan); the practical movement of people (van der Kloof) and goods (Cox & Rzewnicki); or in communicative travel through the social networks, online and in real space that connect riding activities within subcultures (Bunte). The chapters, therefore, reflect a concern not with the spectacle of diversity, but with the complexities of social life and social practice signalled by such self-evident diversity.

Cycling – or perhaps it should more accurately be "cyclings" – take(s) place in physical spaces, mapped out, shaped and routed. These routes may be shared with other mobile subjects, may echo with historical reference to those who have ridden the same terrains before, or may simply be mundane, unconsidered roads of quotidian travel. The qualities

4

of space are such that layers of meaning are not inherent, but culturally produced: the roads of the monumental Paris-Brest-Paris ride described by Bunte are simultaneously the ordinary tarmac of the French national roads system.

As noted previously, the authorship of this volume reflects conversations between very different experiential worlds of cycling, the core contrast being between the UK and the Netherlands. During the later 1950s and 1960s, rates of urban bicycle travel dropped dramatically in both countries, in common with many other northern European nations (de la Bruhèze & Veraart, 1999; Oldenziel & de la Bruhèze, 2009). But policy responses in the two were very different. While Britain concentrated on the growth of "the great car economy", the Netherlands sought to revitalize the place of cycling in its transport culture. It drew on historic national identifications of the Netherlands as a cycling nation to justify policies of investment (Ebert, 2004; Schwanen et al., 2004). In the UK, cycling persisted largely through sports and recreation. Consequently, most British cities lack the dedicated infrastructure for cycling that was implemented in the Netherlands. Often, where pedestrianization schemes were introduced into British cities in the 1970s they served to make cycling even more difficult. Much of the UK recovery of cycling through the 1980s and 1990s was as a leisure pursuit and took place in spaces other than the public highway. Persistent campaigning has localized impacts, but little consistent or coherent national policy has ensued. Britain has seen some degree of resurgence in transport cycling over the past decade, but as a highly localized phenomenon, with London as flagship. But even the best UK cities struggle to provide a systemic approach to welcoming provision for transport cycling. Consequently, to ride a bicycle in the Netherlands today is to be integrated into a normal, unconsidered everyday practice. The bicycle is simply a tool for getting around. In the UK, by contrast, the bike represents a lifestyle choice: riding as transport a deliberate act, which in most situations will result in contesting occupation of public highways with motorized road users (Lenting, 2014). Alternatively, as Pooley et al., (2013, p. 150) put it: "cycling is a relatively popular form of recreation across contemporary Britain, but as a mode of urban transport it is virtually irrelevant". Dedicated cycling infrastructure provision may not necessarily produce higher levels of urban utility cycling, but lack of it can be a profound deterrent. Connected to these contrasting positions the issue of status distinguishes different approaches to cycling and the meanings it invokes. For van der Kloof's adult learners in this volume, learning to ride has a positive status impact. Pooley et al.'s study (2013) found that cycling was associated with low social status, or that it was seen as simply being a childhood activity to be left behind.

By taking the title *Cycling Cultures*, then, this volume is not simply attempting to chronicle the variety of practices to which the title of cycling can be attached, but to point towards the manner in which social practices are bound up with meaning-making. In relation to the second of those two terms in the title, Bauman, in the introduction to the 2003 edition of his *Culture as Praxis* (1973, p. xv ff.), points to the ambivalence that the idea of culture constantly inhabits. It is poised, he argues – consonant with Raymond Williams' work on the topic (see discussion in Chapter 1 of this volume) – between two poles. First, culture exists in reference to activities of freedom, of self-defining creativity. The second pole is that of routinized social ordering, just as anthropology traditionally uses the concept of culture to specify that which defines deviance against routinized cultural norms. If we locate the bodily practice of cycling within this ambivalence we perhaps can have a clearer explanation of the tension between two poles of cycling's public presentation. On the one hand, there are the cultural images of cycling promoted in advertising campaigns (for everything from holiday cottages and wine bottles to insurance policies) with their clear promises of freedom and liberation from routine. These liberatory images are shared within much of the magazine press devoted to the celebration of leisure cycling activities. On the other hand, there is the reality of the vast majority of everyday, quotidian riding for transport. Routes and times are constrained by the routines of everyday life and journeys regulated by urban infrastructure, which can be described in terms of a regulatory regime designed to produce a disciplined subject (Bonham & Cox, 2010).

The task of beginning to unpack the relationship between theories of culture and practices of cycling provides the theme of the opening chapter of the book. It brings together an assessment of the diversity of cycling practices as seen through a number of lenses provided by social theory. It then turns around the gaze to ask not how cycling advocacy may be viewed as a social movement, but what the consequences and implications of viewing it as such might be for the advocacy movement itself. These themes are also revisited in the final chapter which re-examines the questions posed by the intervening contributions.

In her chapter, Ida Sabelis considers how the very ordinariness of the bicycle as a transport choice in the Netherlands can actually render it invisible despite its ubiquity. Whereas the resurgence of Dutch cycling in the 1970s was brought about by concerted policy intervention (Stoffers, 2012), the very success of these processes four decades on risks losing grasp of the mechanisms needed to bring about change. Moreover, normative assumptions about what it means to travel and about the travelling body become problematic for those who do not, for whatever reason, conform to those norms. A process of "othering" takes place. Applying insights developed in the sociology of diversity and applied in business, she shows how these barriers, physical and conceptual, might be overcome. Thus, the chapter is also illustrative of the diversity

7

of analytical approaches and models found within the social sciences themselves. Whilst not explicitly discussed in the chapter, it is worth noting that the manner in which the topic is explored here typifies work emerging from the mobilities field in that it is clearly indebted to postcolonial and feminist theory for its framing of the problematic and in the search for solutions. Similar underlying theoretical perspectives can also be seen in the chapter from Angela van der Kloof.

A striking contrast is provided by Horton and Jones in their contribution. Here, two researchers involved with the *Understanding Walking and Cycling* project demonstrate the consequences of the very different legacy of transport policy on cycling in England. With the notable exceptions of a few cities, there are few gains to be lost. To ride is a marginal and negligible activity, but even within these very small numbers there is profound diversity, largely ignored in policy making. The argument of these two authors is a powerful one: the structures of normalized expectations are such that transforming patterns of mobility cannot just be about cycle promotion but requires analysis of the structures that currently serve to maintain a car-based mobility system. Here they draw attention to the ideological dimensions of culture, and the conflicts that are inherent in any challenges to current arrangements of power and the vested interests by which they are supported.

The next chapter, moving the focus back to the Netherlands, further illustrates the contrasts between the two nations in terms of practice, but it also highlights the commonality of ideological conflict. Van der Kloof writes specifically from her own experiences as a cycle trainer, understanding how cycling behaviours can be shaped by cultural norms and experiences that may be nothing to do with cycling itself. To plan interventions whilst being sensitive to cultural preconceptions is revealed as a complex task that demands sensitivity and patience. Provision of adequate infrastructure and even the presence of dominant narratives of everyday travel behaviour that normalize cycling are not enough to enable individual cycling practices without further encouragement. Her chapter demonstrates potential disconnection between macro-level assumptions about intervention and the micro-level attention to the cultural dimensions that shape individual life. To assume that we are all independent agents of choice, working within a frame of free-floating rationality over our decision-making process is to miss the embeddedness and sociality of existing lives. Yet simultaneously, her narrative demonstrates that such embeddedness should not be essentialized. Actions are still contingent and open to change, but the constructions of those behaviours may need to be understood differently. Finally, she makes the important observation that practices in the formation of cycling cultures and in the enculturation of cycling can also be affected by policy considerations beyond the obvious factors, in this case those to do with immigration, not transport.

Brian Deegan writes from the perspective of a sociologically trained planner and engineer, working to find measures that can reflect and be sensitive to different needs in a concrete situation. Taking mapping as the focus, his chapter emphasizes the need to employ appropriate methods in order to generate data beyond any prior assumptions. By making a discursive analysis of the mapping processes, he explores the normative discourse employed by mapmakers, and the assumptions underpinning what might outwardly be considered a neutral and objective process. While the specificities of London wayfinding form the central element of the investigation, the processes revealed in Deegan's focus groups can be replicated in any other cities.

Where the first four chapters take a broader view on the diversity and how to manage it, the latter chapters in this volume explore the specificities of particular types of riding. The chapter by Peter Cox and Randy Rzewnicki combines the two perspectives of a sociologist of cycling and the insights of someone centrally involved in practical project management in relation to the object of study. Examining the changing uses and fortunes of cargo bikes demonstrates how some aspects of cycling exist as functions of other sectors of the economy. Use of the cargo bike has been profoundly tied to changes in the shape of retail and the relation of the retail sector to its customer base. What had virtually disappeared by the mid 1970s, re-emerged as part of a counter-culture arguing for a different mode of economy and society. In the past decade, digital technologies and energy prices have once more reshaped the retail sector and rendered new strategic importance to logistics. An older technology is now recycled to become once more a vital part of the urban mobility landscape, for both domestic and commercial uses.

Heike Bunte's chapter on randonneuring is a study of a very particular and relatively exclusive set of cycling practices, albeit a very longstanding one. These rides and riders fall into a category of activity that might well be called serious organized leisure. The riders do not compete against others, strictly speaking: it is ultimately only the self that is challenged in the long hours of long-distance riding. Every finisher within the time limit gets the same ultimate accolade. Energy resources and resourcefulness itself are the prime qualities required of those who take part in this specialist subculture. At another level, her chapter highlights the importance of thinking about cycling in rhythms. The cyclical repetition of the pedalling body, coupled with the linear travel through space, engage a dialogue of space and time echoing Lefebvre (2004). She stresses the importance that these riders place in finding their own individual rhythms and the constant pace. No place here for the sudden accelerations and attacks of racing, or the stop-start rhythms of urban commuting, but long hours of self-constrained, and self-contained relentlessness. Perhaps the only other parallel in the

Introduction

Anglophone world is the similarly little-explored experience of the long-distance (twelve- and twenty-four hour) time triallist.

By narrowing our gaze to a specific case study, the final illustrative chapter on women cyclists in the British CTC (Cyclists' Touring Club) allows us to show the degree to which roles and norms can vary tremendously over time. Perhaps counter-intuitively, the 1930s are revealed as a decade in which opportunities for women opened up and the social definitions of their roles became more malleable. Cycle touring is exposed as a means through which change could be forged. Yet it is also clear that the gains were opportunistic and as social structures changed in the 1950s, so the gains of the 1930s were all but forgotten. The study can also be read in conjunction with van der Kloof's chapter, to remind ourselves how rapidly attitudes and practices can change. Cycling is a cultural phenomenon but one that reveals how malleable cultural traits are, rather than essential. Perhaps we may conclude that studying cultures of cycling informs us both about the practices of cycling and the construction of cultural identities.

A single volume such as this can only provide a tiny set of windows into such a complex world. Thinking about cycling as a cultural practice, we begin to open up the space to think not simply about a singular activity but a range of diverse, even disconnected practices that may be read through a range of different lenses. Connecting the individual chapters together, in different ways, and reading them against one another assists in thinking through the issues of complexity and diversity in cycling, and we hope shows how these can contribute to the bigger processes of change in which we are all involved.

References

Bauman, Z. (2003 [1973]). *Culture as Praxis*. Cambridge, UK: Polity Press.

Bonham, J., & Cox, P. (2010). The Disruptive Traveller? A Foucauldian Analysis of Cycleways. *Road & Transport Research 19*(2), 43–54.

de la Bruhèze, A., & Veraart, F.C.A. (1999). *Fietsverkeer in Praktijk en Beleid in de Twintigste Eeuw: Overeenkomsten en Verschillen in het Fietsgebruik te Amsterdam, Eindhoven, Enschede, Zuid-Oost Limburg, Antwerpen, Manchester, Kopenhagen, Hannover en Basel*. The Hague, Netherlands: Ministerie van Verkeer en Waterstaat.

Ebert, A.-K. (2004). Cycling Towards the Nation: The Use of the Bicycle in Germany and the Netherlands, 1880–1940. *European Review of History. 11*(3): 347–364.

Horton, D., Rosen, P., & Cox, P. (eds.) (2007). *Cycling and Society* Farnham, UK: Ashgate Publishing.

Lefebvre, H. (2004). Rhythmanalysis: Space, Time and Everyday Life [trans. S. Elden & G. Moore]. London, UK: Continuum.

Lenting, H. (2014). Comparison of Intrinsic Motivations for Cycling. Unpublished Bachelor's Thesis, Leeuwarden, Netherlands. http://goo.gl/ eeTjun [accessed 3 November 2014].

Oldenziel, R., & de la Bruhèze, A. (2011). Contested Spaces: Bicycle Lanes in Urban Europe, 1900–1995. *Transfers. 1*(2), 31–49.

Pooley, C., Jones, T., Tight, M., Horton, D., Scheldeman, G., Jopson, A., & Strano, E. (2013). *Promoting Walking and Cycling: New Perspectives on Sustainable Travel*. Bristol, UK: Policy Press.

Schwanen, T., Dijst, M., & Dielman, F. (2004). Policies for Urban Form and Their Impact on Travel: The Netherlands Experience. *Urban Studies, 41*, 579–603.

Stoffers, M. (2012). Cycling as Heritage: Representing the History of Cycling in the Netherlands. *Journal of Transport History*, 33(1), 92–114.

Urry, J. (2008). Moving on the Mobility Turn. In W. Canzler, V. Kaufmann, & S. Kesselring (eds.), *Tracing Mobilities: Towards a Cosmopolitan Perspective* (pp. 13–24). Farnham, UK: Ashgate Publishing.

CHAPTER 1

CYCLING CULTURES AND SOCIAL THEORY

Peter Cox

The single term "cycling" covers a huge variety of activities, by different groups of people, in different places and for different purposes. In the title of this volume it is coupled to "culture", which Raymond Williams (1976, p. 87) described as "one of the two or three most complicated words in the English language". Together they form a daunting pairing, perhaps almost so entangled as to become unintelligible. In order to make sense of the title, and of the underlying themes of the book, this opening chapter considers what they might mean when analysed together through the lenses of the social sciences. The chapter falls into two parts. Firstly, it considers definitional problems associated with thinking about cycling cultures. It introduces some ways of thinking that enable a clearer interpretation and disaggregation of the various activities that are described as cultures of cycling. The latter part of the chapter takes analytical frameworks for understanding culture and power and uses them to examine how insights from social theory can inform the practices of specific pro-cycling activism that seek to promote cycling as a sustainable transport choice. Although contrasting approaches, these two tasks are linked in their concern to understand both the mundane reality of diverse cycling cultures and the implications that this diversity has in cycle promotion.

Cycling: the act of riding a "cycle". Cycling? Bicycling? Tricycling? Which, or all of these are appropriate? Which begs a further question – when is a bicycle not a bicycle? These questions may seem pedantic, but we live in a world where we crave definition and degrees of distinction, if only in order to be able to navigate our way through it with any meaning. The

United Nations Convention on Road Traffic (1968, p. 5) provides an international legal definition: "'Cycle' means any vehicle which has at least two wheels and is propelled solely by the muscular energy of the persons on that vehicle, in particular by means of pedals or hand-cranks". We can see here some basic principles at work. A cycle is a tool for movement. It is propelled in whole or in part by human motive power. Perhaps it might also be useful to distinguish between two forms of this propulsion, those that involve some form of linkage between the human body and the machine (for example pedals and treadles), and those that can simply be scooted along. Additionally, other sources of power may be added to augment, or even ultimately supplant the human input, at which stage, it may be safely regarded as a motor vehicle. The relationship of cycles to other vehicles is discussed in Cox & Van De Walle (2007) and need not concern us overmuch here. Suffice to say that the demarcation between motorized and non-motorized vehicles is a lot more porous than most current legal definitions allow, and that the implications of this for future sustainable mobility scenarios are extensive. To summarize the elements of cycle design that do concern us here, the cycle is a technology that produces increased mobility through the mechanical input of human power.

As machines, cycles require design and production: processes that involve deliberate choice and investment of time and money, political and economic decision making. As manufactured objects, they are traded; they gain and lose value in various sorts of markets. Values are social and economic – both use-value and symbolic-value are involved and may be contradictory. In short, as Vivanco (2013, p. 26) states: "the bicycle is a complex socio-technical object whose meaning and uses are shaped variously through its histories, production and uses". So, while we may describe the bicycle relatively simply in terms of its mechanical qualities as an object, we should also take into account the insights from the sociology of technology (Bijker et al. 2012) that allow us to understand that technological innovation and production takes place within, and is deeply shaped by, and inextricable from, socio-historical contexts: specific societies with their social structures, politics, and economics.

To use this technology of mobility requires space. A bicycle is only potentially a mobility device until it is ridden. The form that this space should, or does, take can vary tremendously. For example, questions of land ownership, whether or not routes and roads exist, and the local legal constraints on use of roads, rights of way, highways and other spaces all contribute to determining where and how cycling can take place. Relationships to other forms of mobility can be interrogated. What (if any) should be the principle of demarcation of road and route space? By mode of travel (i.e. vehicle type)? By speed? Should certain modes be favoured or disfavoured for social, environmental or economic reasons? Differing presumptions underlie different stances taken in current debates over planning for cycling.

Finally, the act of riding implies a rider. Who uses cycles? How do existing narratives based on class, gender, age and ethnicity shape uses? Does the use of any given technology feed into the creation of collective or personal identity?

The simple definitional statement with which we began seems to spiral into a whole realm of variables, possibilities centred around three key elements of machines, riders, and spaces that together provide an ensemble we call cycling. In order to navigate out of this morass, we can take a number of discrete themes that can help illuminate the practice of cycling and the formation of cultural identities around cycling. Before considering the diversity of riders and riding, let us first turn to the diversity of machinery.

A Diversity of Machinery

The range of cycles available today is perhaps greater than ever. Cycle design ranges far beyond the simple categorizations found in individual manufacturer's catalogues or even in retailers' sales lists. From compact folding cycles, through to Velomobiles and from ultra-lightweight racing recumbents to cargo cycles, there is even a trade show specifically for specialist cycles (http://www.spezialradmesse.de). This variety allows for different activities and different designs have consequences for their use of space in the built environment (Cox, 2007). Hadland and Lessing (2014) provide a fascinating insight into the range of ways that designers and manufacturers have tackled a range of problems over the years. Here is not the place for endless description. What is worth noting, however, is that each design is necessarily confined by a series of parameters that serve to shape the actions of innovators and constructors. For our purposes, we may note four important elements that need to be considered, but that may pose contradictory demands upon designs: *Specific function* (e.g. intermodality, off-road capability); *Carrying capacity* (volume and/or mass, rider(s) and baggage); *Efficiency* of power use; and *Comfort and ease of use.*

Designing for a specific function, whether cargo carrying or the ability to fold (so as to be portable as luggage on a train, for example) may be uppermost in the constructor's consideration, but the degree to which this specialized function is met can impact upon the other functions. A time trial machine built for racing within the specific regulatory restrictions of international cycle sport can afford to be uncomfortable and hard to use, as long as it is sufficiently efficient in its specific role. The more specific the role, however, the less versatile it may be: the time trial machine is little use beyond its specific athletic discipline. Most machines for more general use, however, require compromises to be made between conflicting demands. A cycle designed to fold for intermodal travel on the other hand, needs to be light enough to carry when folded, but this portability should not compromise the riding qualities, since it is also required to be used for general transport purposes, and will probably need some means to carry the usual everyday luggage.

Efficiency might initially seem to be solely the concern of the racer or the engineer, but has significant implications in other uses. The less strong and less fit the rider, the more important is the efficient use of the limited power input. The less energy available for cycling, the more important it is to use that capacity efficiently so as to make it less arduous. Efficiency has a number of components including weight, rolling resistance, air resistance (Wilson, 2004; Burrows, 2004). Without going deeply into the engineering factors, it remains an obvious truism that gains in one area inevitably mean compromises in another.

Human power for cycling can be augmented in several ways. Adding a motor creates a hybrid machine. This can be either as a human–electric hybrid, or as a human–internal combustion engine hybrid, using very low-power motors. Although popular prior to the late 1950s, these latter are not currently legal in Europe. Such hybrids can increase versatility, but at a cost in other areas. Adding extra power is a logical and rational response especially for those who do not see (or want to see) themselves as particularly athletic or who are limited in strength. The second obvious application is when moving large masses of freight. The appropriate amount of power to add, and in what form, is an area for considerable debate, and experimentation.

Even before we consider the interaction of these diverse technologies with their riders, we can see that this is a complicated problem. What a cyclist is depends in part on what the cycle is. One way of thinking about just this element is depicted in Figure 1.1. This model sketches the relationships between some of the range of cycles around: some familiar, some less so. They are organized around the three axes of carrying capacity, efficiency and power. It is not designed to be a comprehensive model and it is open to considerable revision (for example, other axes such as versatility might be employed). Rather, it provides a way of thinking through what we are doing and what affordances are created by different technological possibilities which may allow different segments of the populations to ride.

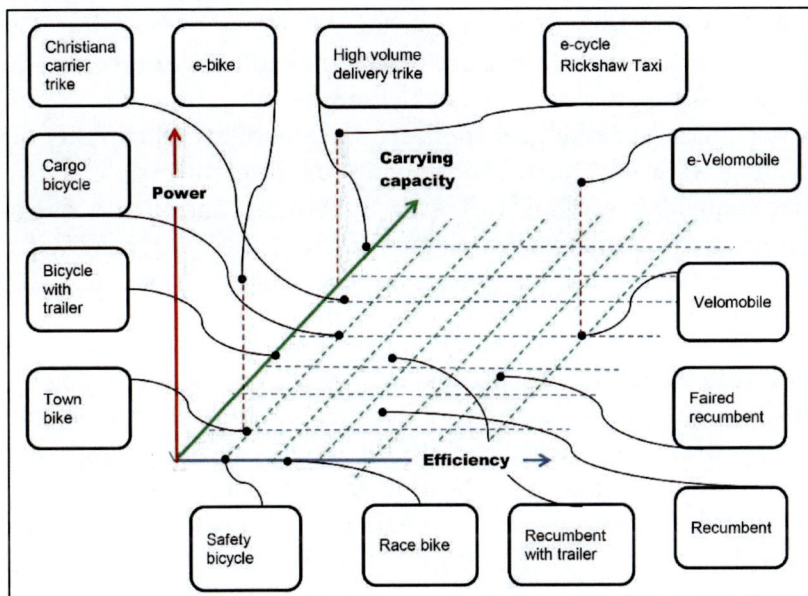

Figure 1.1. Three-dimensional grid mapping of the relationship between different types of bicycle.

Different technologies facilitate different practices. A single rider may engage in multiple practices as their needs and requirements change. We should not think of a single person as a user of only one technology. Cycle users, especially those using more specialist machines may have a selection of machines (tools) to use for different purposes. Each of the technologies has its own "affordances": that is, it allows different actions to be undertaken. Designs have different space-use requirements, not just those arising from the physical size. For example, rates of acceleration and deceleration and braking characteristics will vary according to the mass being moved and the design of the braking system. Turning circles and parking space requirements change with differently shaped cycles. Complex flows of cycle traffic with mixed characteristics need more space than uniform processions all going at the same pace. All these factors have implications for the building of environments of cycling. Conversely, the built environment will shape the experiences and practices undertaken within it.

Diverse technologies are the first element in the diversity of cycling cultures. Our social diversity as different people, ages, sizes and shapes, ethnicities, men and women and fitness levels produces a diversity of capacities. Each of these interacts with our variety of technologies to produce a kaleidoscopic image of cycling, ever shifting and unpredictable.

Social Practices and Identities
As we go further, however, it is valuable to consider the relationships that may exist between using a cycle (cycling) and being a cyclist. Horton & Parkin (2013) point to the inverse relationship between the prevalence of a cycling and its contribution to the formation of a specific identity around that practice (see also Vivanco, 2013, p. 14; Lenting, 2014).

In the UK, to ride a cycle of any description for everyday transport is to be part of a tiny minority, as low as 1% of travellers (or fewer). When one is part of a visible minority, identity matters. A sense of belonging to and realizing a collective identity legitimizes the isolated individual. It binds them to a broader reality. This identification works both ways. It comes from external sources as well. The 80% of staff who arrive at work by car (at my home university in the UK) are not identified as "the drivers" whereas the 1% who arrive by bike are classified and get referred to as "cyclists". The reality of the situation is that cycle commuting is so rare that I know almost every rider on my route to work by sight and almost every member of academic staff at the university who rides regularly. In contrast, at the research institute in Munich where I write these words, cycling to work is so unremarkable as to be not worthy of comment. It is just a way of getting to the office, whether by the most junior intern or the institute director. They neither consider themselves "cyclists" nor consider their commuting practice as worthy of mention. Indeed, to describe oneself as a cyclist implies a kind of enthusiasm bordering on fanaticism or fetishism.

As minority riders however, we allow and even embrace this collective identity because it offers us solidarity. It offers security and protection. It assures us that we are each not just isolated deviants. It can even offer leverage to be seen as part of a significant minority. In C. Wright Mills' (1959) expression, it allows the personal troubles we may individually encounter as cyclists, to be transformed into social issues. Simultaneously, we also should acknowledge that this collectivity is – adopting Benedict Anderson's (2006) term as it has been re-employed in social movement studies – an "imagined" community: an artificial grouping forged of convenience not a pre-existing empirical object (Melucci, 1996). Though cycle commuters, wherever they are, may acknowledge, even recognize each other and say hello as we pass on the morning journey, we have little or nothing in common with each other, save a mode of locomotion. The term "cyclist", signifies little more than "shoe-wearer". It is a true depiction of common practice, but the term only becomes meaningful if it refers to something more. Is there really anything that we share, culturally speaking?

What makes imagined communities meaningful for any minority group identified as a group, is their shared marginality, often the shared confrontation of an externally hostile world, a shared oppression. To be a "cyclist" in the UK

21

is to recognize that one shares a minority practice confronted on a regular basis by hostility from dominant masses of road users in cars. The term "cyclist" is therefore a political necessity for survival, but still an imagined unity.

To understand any further, we need to disaggregate the practice itself. We need to think about the diversity of practices, of users, of the variety of technologies that combine with our diverse population to make an even more complex and ever changing kaleidoscope image of cyclists. (After all a cycle without a rider is merely one more item of clutter, and a bicycle rider without a bicycle is ... not a cyclist.)

To explore the diversity of cycling practices we can first consider the variety of activities and behaviours that may be conjured up by the term, irrespective of the identity of the rider. Cycling activities are normally divided up by journey purpose: as utility, leisure, sport. These are our more familiar categories with which both manufacturers and policy makers work. But these are only arbitrary categories, we can think of other ways that are more appropriate to depict the diversity. Trip-chaining and multi-functional journeys are recognized as common phenomena that disrupt this trip purpose analysis in other forms of transport study and planning, but rarely in relation to cycling. In an earlier study (Cox, 2005) I argued for a more complex differentiation of leisure that distinguished between "play" and "organised leisure". The difference between these two categories is the goal orientation of the latter and its emphasis on the acquisition of skills associated with the practice in whichever form it takes. Cycling as play allows the activity to be important in and of itself, particularly since this is the first form of riding that most encounter. It may also be a means to other goals, such as family bonding. Whether bicycle users change to other modes of cycling or not, the ludic element is not to be dismissed lightly, especially as it has the capacity to underpin all subsequent riding, as is particularly visible in

22

literary memoirs and reflections on cycling (see e.g. Bobet, 2008). Rather than there being a clear conceptual division between sport, leisure and utility riding, therefore, we can see a continuum of activity in which riders occupy different positions at different times.

Coupled with this spectrum of activity, Figure 1.2 was employed to map the range of meanings and values that were attached to cycles and cycling. This was devised in conjunction with cyclists interviewed, and was used to help think about both machinery and rides. What became clear through fieldwork discussions, and is illustrated by the two axes in the chart, is that people not only behave in different ways when they ride, but also understand their activities and technologies in different ways. These can vary for a single person as occasions and practices change, as will be illustrated in the next section.

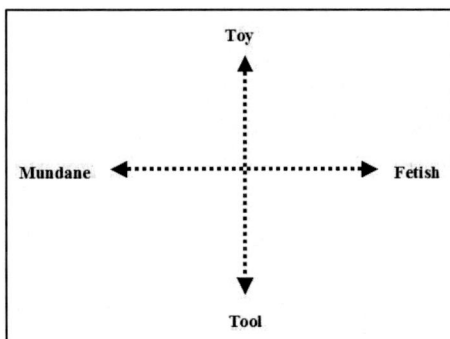

Figure 1.2. Attitudes to the bicycle and the ride.

Unpacking the Practice

A more general framework for understanding social practices examines the interaction of three elements found in every practice: competences, meanings and materials (Shove et al., 2012).

- Competences. The skills and abilities brought to bear or required by an activity

23

- Meanings. The range of meanings, symbolic and significatory understood by the practitioner and those conveyed to the outside world by the action. Also those meanings imputed by observers of the practice
- Materials. Not only the technologies of the bicycle itself in its myriad forms, but also the range of assorted infrastructures and technologies of space in which to ride – the materiality of space.

Most importantly, these elements are interrelated and interact: change the technology of the bicycle and it may require different competences and acquire different meanings, as described above. The easiest way to demonstrate this is by thinking through some different journeys (without changing the rider). These scenarios can enable us to think about the changing construction of a practice, from perspectives of both actor and observer.

Monday morning. Raining again. Off to work. A pile of marking and several textbooks to take back to the office. The extra weight doesn't really matter, keeping dry does, so the raincoat and trousers to keep my work clothes dry are the most important. The material technology of the bike, its step-through design, lights to cut through the gloom and mudguards are all designed to make this stop-start journey easy. Speed is not an issue but as I arrive, I am signalling my own competence as a cycle-traveller by arriving dry (unlike others who have got wet at the bus stop or walking from the car!). But the knowledge of what is needed to arrive in this state, and the material technologies to enable this are the result of experience. The interplay between competences and technologies is mediated through experience and the affordances of my status as a middle-class professional with sufficient income to economically afford these choices. The technologies deployed signal different things to different people, depending on their own journeys and experiences.

24

The same journey in the bright sunshine of a summer morning is altered. Its meaning shifts radically. Instead of comments of pity or admiration of my hardiness from co-workers, it evokes comments that might even border on jealousy over the half an hour I have already spent outside enjoying the morning sunshine before the working day starts. I can choose to increase the resentment by talking about the herons, cormorants and other birds spotted on the tidal riverside as I rode to work. These sets of meanings are also dependent upon the place I work, the patterns of journeying in this city, this nation.

Another day, I take out my carbon-frame race bike. Its minimally lightweight and low rolling resistance urge me to wear cycle specific clothing, close fitting so it doesn't flap in the wind and minimizes air resistance. Clipping into the pedals, it feels like putting on a pair of gloves. It provokes me to accelerate rapidly and go looking for hills to climb, nodding my connection to the local sporting club-riders out on the road. I don't want to be on the separated cycle path designed for riding at much slower speeds and shared with pedestrians and dog-walkers. When I am in this guise, they transform from fellow travellers to potential threats. The material technology allows my speed and gives me tremendous enjoyment simply revelling in the experience of movement.

But this technology also has its constraints. It is useless when anything needs to be carried. When I wave a friendly hello to a fellow "cyclist" going to the shops on her town bike to buy a newspaper, it only produces a look of baffled bewilderment: "who is this and why are they waving at me?". The meaning is ambiguous not inherent. The ride shows off my competences – my relative fitness – knowing that other racing cyclists will subtly (or not so subtly) make sure I "deserve" or have "earned the right" to be riding the cycling equivalent of a Ferrari.

The practice of cycling can therefore be understood in the interplay of competences, meanings and materials. Each of us can think about our own and/or others' cycling and not-cycling behaviours, what we ride (or don't), for what different reasons. What we project in our practices, what competences and experiences are required to undertake this ride – from the choice of bicycle we have made, to the clothing we wear and the sense of self that is invoked or produced. We choose for different reasons, not just what we want to do, but also who do we want to be? We constantly re-create kaleidoscopic patterns of diversity.

The interplay of competences, meanings and materials is also context-reliant. Take me away from the context of my home town in the UK and these identities, with their subtle shifts and conveyances of meaning, matter far less. In some places, for example, I become just another bicycle rider: one of thousands, whichever cycle I choose. In the context of urban transport, the race bike which is so much a joy on long, open roads is even somewhat absurd, like using a Ferrari to do the shopping. My level of competency can also change, depending on the context of riding. Unfamiliar streets and unknown local habits of moving in traffic, or riding in unfamiliar terrains can impute new sets of meanings and emotions attached to the same overall practice.

Yet beyond this variability we can also see clusters of shared identities and meanings begin to emerge around shared practices: the beginnings of what can be called cultural identities. Practices may be diverse but they are also visible in clustered form. Shared experiences and narratives, through face-to-face, social media or print communication create clusters of common knowledge for which the language of culture seems appropriate. Although there is much more to be said about the role of space in cycling, sufficient mention has been made in the foregoing to indicate its essential contribution to the formations of identities and cycling cultures, without devoting further discussion to it. For the moment we can move on to think about the cultural dimension of practices and begin the transition to the second part of the chapter, moving from a descriptive interpretation of cycling cultures, to an analysis of the implications of thinking theoretically about cycling cultures in cycle promotion.

Culture and Subcultures

Despite the complexity of the language of culture, Williams (1976) nevertheless distinguished three main strands of use which intertwine but can be differentiated.

- A general process of intellectual, spiritual and aesthetic development.
- A particular way of life, whether of a people, a period or a group.
- The works and practices of intellectual, and especially artistic, activity (i.e. signifying practices).

It is the middle of these categories, reflecting a growing ethnographic and anthropological interest in social scientific investigations of cycling that is generally employed when discussing cultures of cycling (e.g. Aldred & Jungnickel, 2012). The significance of Williams' thinking about culture and society, however, is that it is rooted in consideration of its relationship to power, a theme he developed over the years. As an analysis of the relationship of culture and power, we can make a shift from the previously largely descriptive insights of the variety of activities that might be described as cultures of cycling, to a more analytical understanding of the role of cultural identity and practice in processes of social change.

Williams wrote against a background of twentieth-century social elites fearful of the appearance and growth of various forms of mass culture. The emergence of mass culture, as a feature of mass society, was contrasted with the maintenance of social elites as a safeguard against barbarism, (*pace* Arnold, 1869). Practices of the mass population were understood as inimical to the preservation of high culture from the second quarter of the twentieth century, rendering those activities of ordinary working class citizens (the social majority) as inherently undesirable. The practical upshots of this fear in relation to the bicyclist can be seen in this letter from *Car and Golf* (Spring 1926):

> The cyclist is commonly supposed to be a poor man, a man of the working classes, a Trade Unionist in other words, and to compel him to carry a red lamp would not increase the popularity of any government, it would not bring any additional revenue to the treasury, and it might possibly be used by the Trade Unions and other political bodies as a club with which to belabour any government that introduces such legislation.

Where cycling was the transport choice and practice of the many, this rendered it vulnerable to elitist suspicion.

Williams' work stands as part of a new wave of critical voices from the 1950s onwards, re-examining cultural practices and identities to counter these assumptions. In the UK these voices coalesced in the Centre for Contemporary Cultural Studies at the University of Birmingham. For our purposes, out of the vast range of work arising from this source, the most valuable for our study here is work on subcultures, which provides a number of observations that can be used to help understand cycling through a cultural lens.

While subcultural study has taken various forms and directions (see Williams, 2011), Gelder usefully notes that subcultures can be distinguished as the narratives of groups, "that are in some way represented as non-normative or marginal through their particular interests and practices, through what they are, what they do and where they do it" (2005, p. 1). Through the second half of the twentieth century, European nations became dominated by structures of auto-mobility (Urry, 2007). That is, the norms of mobility practices were, and in most cases remain, shaped around private motoring, irrespective of whether it is numerically predominant. Therefore, in all but a few specific territories and times, cycling in Europe can therefore be understood as a sub-cultural activity inasmuch as it stands outside the mainstream "normative" practices of society.

Pursuing Gelder's definition further, we can make a distinction between marginality and non-normativity. The former indicates a level of separation from the main flow of the culture and practice of a society. Usually, it is associated with distinctive difference from the majority practice or identity of a society. Being on the edge of the mainstream of thought or practice is frequently a useful indicator of one's relationship to power within a given society. However, analysis of social class, and especially of the power and role of elites (see e.g. Mills, 1956; Miliband, 1984) can ensure that numeric majorities may not command effective control or representation in relation to decision making over their future or constraints on their current actions. Small numbers of elites, by virtue of privileged access to the instruments of economic political and social power, control the capacity to create and maintain normative discourses. Normativity – the capacity to establish and police social, legal and political norms – is therefore separate from numerical dominance.

But this does not mean total dominance by structures of power. Spaces of resistance constantly open even within the most apparently closed systems (McKay, 1996). In the context of making change, bell hooks (1990) recognizes marginality specifically as a site of resistance, a conceptual space within which critique can emerge and be nurtured (this link to multicultural feminist studies will be returned to later in the discussion). The margin is not just the space (physical in the case of much road cycling) to which one is confined, but also a vital resource for the formation of resistant counter-culture. Being distanced from centres of power provides critical distance, allowing the formation of perspectives and allowing analysis that is impossible from the centre.

In the case of cycling, historical research shows that in the UK, for example, even when cyclists were the physical majority of road users in the 1930s, road policy was still formed around the interests of the promotion of motor traffic (Cox, 2012). Cyclists were not marginalized numerically, but they were marginalized discursively. In other words, though a majority, their voice was not normative: it was not assumed to be paramount in planning and development. Instead, the voices of the minority (private motor-vehicle owners) were prioritized. Practically, this resulted in cyclists being pushed out of policy discussions on the future of roads. Majority power is not an automatic correlate of numerical superiority.

One uniting factor bringing cyclists together at local, national and even international levels since the very earliest days of cycling, has been the formation of clubs and other formal associations (for example, the Cyclists' Touring Club (CTC) in the UK was formed in 1878). Almost from the beginning, these clubs, especially as national associations, had both an inward support and social function, coupled with an outward, representative function. Although the CTC was originally formed from the social elite as a means to preserve and replicate their privilege, by the 1930s it recognized the need for broader representation. This latter rapidly grew into a lobbying function developing advocacy for cyclists' rights, whether as tourists, facilitating travel across international borders, or in more specific campaigning for rights on the roads and in other interactions with other forms of mobility. In this example, we see a very clear imagined community formed around shared concern but also creating its own cultural identity through shared practices and common communication. Importantly, these shared practices are not only governed through regulations relating to the use of roads and the public spaces in which they travel, but also through the normative discourses of the broader society. To summarize, we can note that the normative assumptions concerning mobility reflect power elites rather than mass practices. These may coincide, but not necessarily so.

The second insight from subcultural studies is that the further the distance from the norms of society a subculture is, the more important the role of distinctive identity formation and maintenance, as noted above. For cycling advocacy this point is of fundamental importance. Advocacy groups for any community are usually formed by those marginalized from mainstream policy discourse, and in territories in which cycling is a relatively marginal and minority activity, the formation of distinct identities as "cyclists" has been both necessary and pivotal. This is not to homogenize "the cyclist". Indeed cyclist subcultures frequently exhibit multiple (even recursive) frag-mentation into ever smaller sub-groups with particularly clear demarcations, perhaps only visible to "insiders". One may think here of the distinctions between transport, leisure, touring, road and mountain biking, and within these other specific grouping such as fixies, cross-country and downhill. These differen-tiations may be a gift and sometimes a creation of marketing – a business strategy to maximize sales through the artificial creation of identities, but also reflect differences of practice and usage regardless of machine types or styles. Yet through national organizations, all these varied practices can be potentially united in a singular identity.

The third important observation arising from observation and analysis is that subcultures, once defined, frequently perpetuate their own continued distance from the mainstream. The obvious reason is the need to preserve and maintain themselves in the face of mainstream opposition. The perpetuation of a distinctive identity serves as a necessary survival strategy in the face of opposition. However, the corollary of continued opposition is two-fold. On the one hand, the perpetuation of distinctiveness serves to maintain marginalization. It is difficult for oppositional groups to make the transformation into decision-making groups. This can be illustrated clearly in relation to the transformation of green political movements in a number of European nations through the 1980s and 1990s. Access to power and electoral success produced internal division and splits as some sought to maintain distinctiveness, accusing those who argued that they needed to work within the mainstream of political discourse of "selling out" and feeling betrayed by them. A break between idealism and pragmatism became visible. A similar tension can be seen for example in the UK as sport cycling rapidly shifts in the twenty-first century from being largely ignored to achieve iconic status on the back of international sporting success. Talking to longstanding cyclists, it is possible to identify some who are resentful of this new-found popularity and the possibilities of working with systems of governance. For cycling advocacy, awareness is needed of the very real tensions at work. Both perspectives are legitimate and the stakes are not simply matters of intellectual assent, but of personal and collective identity.

On the other hand, continued marginalization may crucially enable a greater level of critique to be developed. What is so good about the mainstream that one should want to join it so much, runs the argument. Distance from the centre is essential because what is under challenge is the very idea of a centre, not just its location. Marginalization, in bell hooks' argument, is the site through which critical gaze can be developed. This is a central theme of queer theory. The challenge posed by queer theory is not just to change social norms but to undermine the fundamental arrangement by which norms operate to homogenize society and to erase or elide difference. Normalcy itself becomes the focus of critique. Queer theory poses a challenge to cycle advocacy especially in terms of the presentation of cycling as a rational choice for an efficient city. Is the aim of cycle advocacy to encourage greater levels of cycle commuting simply to produce a more efficient capitalism, or is activism for cycling cities conjoined with other forms of social critique? These are questions that the cycling advocacy movement has traditionally not addressed in any serious dimension. However, these are the very questions posed by recent social sciences studies on cycling that cross the border between academia and advocacy, creating what the transport historian Gijs Mom (2011) has called a new "emancipatory" subfield. It is to the way in which social theory can go beyond the interpretation of events and enter into dialogue with the objects of its study that we turn for the final section of this chapter.

Cycling, Radical Social Movements and Multiculturalism

The relationship between academic theory and activism has not always been smooth. Ever since Saul Alinsky (1969, p. ix) wrote that "The word 'academic' is a synonym for irrelevant" in the preface to his *Reveille for Radicals*, the relationship between academic research and activist advocacy has been a troubled one. One of the most powerful sets of responses has been in the field of community organizing and community development, where academic research and community empowerment have gone hand in hand through the processes of participatory research (for a classic response to Alinsky, see Stoeker, 1999 and the On-Line Conference on Community Organizing at http://comm-org.wisc.edu/). In the sociological study of social movements, the relationship between groups working for change and the academics studying them has been particularly acute: a situation that Alinsky was recognizing in his activist manuals (Alinksy, 1969, 1971). Yet, here too, the possibility of fruitful collaboration between the study of activism and activists themselves is clearer in examples such as the Vancouver Citizens' Handbook (http://www.citizenshandbook.org/) and its print expansion as *The Troublemaker's Teaparty* by Charles Dobson (2003).

To explore the relationship between theory and advocacy, this final section takes elements from studies in the social sciences to interrogate the practices of cycling advocacy groups, especially as they use the framework of cycling cultures as a significant element in their presentation of public arguments for increased levels of urban cycling. This is most clearly illustrated in the Velo-city conference 2013 hosted by the city of Vienna, which assembled more than 1,400 international delegates under the title of "The Sound of Cycling – Urban Cycling Cultures" (http://velo-city2013.com/). The level of activity and participation to be seen at such conferences is indicative that what may once have been a subcultural minority activity has now entered mainstream policy debate. National and international organizations are no longer just lobbying on behalf of their members but are now frequently arguing for change on behalf of and affecting those who are currently non-cyclists and thus of whom they are not directly representative (see Horton, 2013; Horton & Parkin, 2012).

Yet the question remains, taking us back to the first part of the chapter. How is the diversity previously indicated adequately (re)presented by organizations that speak for cycling? Is it possible to find ways to unite these diverse practices, experiences and subcultures without traducing or misrepresenting them? Are there grounds for creating political unity amidst diversity without erasing the differences?

Before responding to these, however, it is worth thinking about an underlying question that lurks, often hidden and inarticulate, behind much cycle advocacy – as for many other movements for change – and points towards why theory and academic study may not be as irrelevant as Alinsky suggested. Let us pose it in the form of a series of question and answer slogans for a demonstration (one might substitute a number of different demands depending on the particular campaign target).

> What do we want? – More cycling!
>
> When do we want it? – Now!
>
> Why do we want it? – Errr …

For the first two elements, a degree of consensus is easy to discern if one listens to a variety of advocacy groups internationally. The third question is a frequently unasked one behind numerous calls for social change. The degree to which it remains unarticulated is an indicator that movements for change rely on building pragmatic alliances. Stopping to consider underlying reasons, or even ultimate goals risks damaging often fragile coalitions of interests and identities. Not asking ultimate "why", or "to what ultimate end" questions allows the facade of a unified culture to remain. If the "why" question does get asked it may produce a kaleidoscope of responses reflecting a range of political, pragmatic, cultural and local considerations. A myriad of responses reflect the very diversity discussed above. A study of the cycling advocacy literature from the 1930s to the present day and across a number of locations in Europe and the Americas reveals a bewildering variety of arguments. Indeed, this variety provides a cause for celebration in the programme of the Velo-city conference mentioned above, and is used to bring together campaigners from very different backgrounds. Yet it also poses very real questions: firstly, about long-term solidarity and secondly, about what any particular campaign's long-term aims and vision really are, once one looks beneath the immediate surface demands. This dilemma, as mentioned, is not unique to cycle campaigns and advocacy but can be found in a range of social movements.

Cycling as a Social Movement

The idea of cycling advocacy as a social movement or as integrally linked to the emergence of new social movements was a founding theme of the new "emancipatory" subfield described by Gijs Mom (see Rosen, 2002; Horton, 2006). While social movements studies has developed into a large academic field of study (see e.g. Snow et al., 2004), Herbert Blumer's description from the late 1930s is still a valid starting point for understanding the emancipatory thrust of movements for change. Social movements are, he said, "collective enterprises to establish a new order of life. They have their inception in the condition of unrest, and derive their motive power on one hand from dissatisfaction with the current form of life, and on the other hand, from wishes and hopes for a new scheme or system of living" (Blumer, 1939, p. 199).

What is of particular note is that the archetypal social movements emerging in the twentieth century, the women's movement, gay liberation, the green movement, have each been responsible for developing new emancipatories arising from their shared collective identities and pushing at the boundaries of what currently exists. Seen through these lenses, we should expect cycling as an activist movement not simply to develop arguments concerning the arrangement of urban traffic patterns but also to include more profoundly – politically and socially – transformative elements. In keeping with other social movements, we should not be surprised to find both reformist and revolutionary forms of activity and activism. In almost all broad social movements, we see combinations of those who seek modifications within the existing social system, and those who would radically transform the arrangements of society. Thus not only may we find a diversity of activities, but also a diversity of political dimensions within the movement. Radical action and reform go together in historic movements, not as a distraction from one another but as necessary, vibrant and integral parts of a broader process.

The problem faced by actors within a movement remains: how to build alliances of solidarity between divergent and often conflicting elements without denying their differences. Disparate cycling cultures and subcultures can draw on parallels with other social movements in order to understand the interrelationships of parts. One of the most important and certainly one of the clearest examples of another explicitly emancipatory movement dealing with questions of profound diversity is that of multicultural feminism. While ideas and practices of multiculturalism may be devalued by simply reducing them to the observance of a plural society, or be challenged and undermined by current neo-conservative politics as Modood (2013) argues, it is ever more important to rediscover ways of building solidarity across divisive boundaries of separation and difference without dissolving or ignoring our diverse experiences and identities.

As feminist politics has had to come to terms with the complexity of women's lives and move away from the idea of a universal identity of woman, so we can see parallels to the problem of recognizing the category of "cyclists" while simultaneously recognizing the hollowness and artificiality of the term. As Linda Nicholson argues,

> To give up on the idea that 'woman' has one clearly specifiable meaning does not entail that it has no meaning. Rather, this way of thinking about meaning works upon the assumption that such patterns are found within history and must be documented as such. (Nicholson & Seidman, 1995, p. 61)

What binds diverse and often unconnected experiences together is their shared position of struggle. Connection does not come through similarity but through the diverse struggles in which we participate. Copeland (1996, p. 147) puts it even more clearly: "Difference is the authentic context for interdependence".

Diverse cycling cultures, experiences and identities do not invalidate the idea that groups or campaigns can speak about "cycling" but can explore the possibility of forming a radical cycling movement through the embrace of differences and by choosing to work together. Returning to best illustrations from feminist theory we can perhaps reflect on the work of Chantal Mouffe. She describes how feminist struggles deal with diverse cultural experiences.

> Feminist politics should be understood not as a separate politics designed to pursue the interests of women as women, but rather as the pursuit of feminist goals and aims within the context of a wider articulation of demands. Those goals and aims should consist in the transformation of all the discourses, practices, and social relations where the category 'woman' is constructed in a way that implies subordination. Feminism, for me, is the struggle for the equality of women. But this should not be understood as a struggle for realizing the equality of an empirically definable group with a common essence and identity, women, but rather as a struggle against the multiple forms in which the category 'woman' is constructed in subordination. (Mouffe, 1995, p. 329)

What happens if another identity – such as "cyclist" and "cycling" – is substituted for the terms "woman" and "feminist" in this passage? Can Mouffe's analysis be used for a wider analysis of other forms of marginalized identity? One may argue that the precise social location of women's oppression within the structures of patriarchy is unique and that no substitution is possible, yet it would undermine the strength of her theoretical argument to insist that her basic analysis cannot be generalized.

Therefore, can a study of social theory and cycling cultures be used to arrive at a better understanding of bicycle politics? I would suggest that this is the precise task of applied social theory: to not only assist in a better understanding of existing conditions, but also to engage with the concrete processes of change that are part of the everyday world. To return to the sloganeering, "Why do we want it – because it is part of a shared struggle for a better world", allows a space to recognize the diversity of cycling cultures but also to make the idea of cycling culture meaningful.

References

Aldred, R., & Jungnickel, K. (2012). *Cycling Cultures: Summary of Key Findings and Recommendations* [ESRC funded research project] retrieved from http://www.cyclingcultures.org.uk/Final-report-cycling-cultures.pdf [accessed on 16 April 2013.

Alinsky, S. (1969 [1946]). *Reveille for Radicals.* New York, NY: Vintage Books.

Alinsky S. (1971). *Rules for Radicals.* New York, NY: Vintage Books.

Anderson, B. (2006). *Imagined Communities: Reflections on the Origin and Spread of Nationalism* (Revised and extended). London, UK: Verso.

Arnold, M. (1869). *Culture and Anarchy.* Oxford, UK: Oxford World's Classics.

Bijker, W., Hughes, T., & Pinch, T. (2012). *The Social Construction of Technological Systems: New Directions in the Sociology and History of Technology* (anniversary edition). Cambridge MA: MIT Press.

Blumer, H. (1939). Collective Behavior. In R.E. Park, (ed.). *An Outline of the Principles of Sociology* (pp. 219–280). New York, NY: Barnes and Noble.

Bobet, J. (2008). *Tomorrow, We Ride.* Norwich, UK: Mousehold Press.

Burrows, M. (2004). *Bicycle Design: The Search for the Perfect Machine* (second edition). London, UK: Pedal Press.

Copeland, M.S. (1996). Difference as a Category in Critical Theologies for the Liberation of Women, *Concilium*, 1996(1), 141–151.

Cox, P. (2005). Conflicting Agendas in Selling Cycling. Presentation, Web publication and CD-Rom Conference Proceedings Velo-city 2005, Dublin. Dublin: Dublin City Council, 9 June 2005.

Cox, P. (2007). The Role of Human Powered Vehicles in Sustainable Mobility, *Built Environment, 43*(2), 140–160.

Cox, P. (2012). A Denial of Our Boasted Civilisation: Cyclists' Views on Conflicts over Road Use in Britain, 1926–1935. *Transfers*, 2(3), 4–30.

Dobson, C. (2003). *The Troublemaker's Teaparty: A Manual for Effective Citizen Action.* Gabriola Island, BC, Canada: New Society.

Gelder, K. (2005). Introduction: The Field of Subcultural Studies. In K. Gelder & S. Thornton (eds.), *The Subcultures Reader* (second edition) (pp. 1–15). London, UK: Routledge.

Hadland, T., & Lessing H.-E. (2014). *Bicycle Design: An Illustrated History.* Cambridge MA: MIT Press.

hooks, b. (1990). Marginality as a Site of Resistance. In R. Ferguson, M. Gever, T.T. Minh-ha, & C. West (eds.), *Out There: Marginalization and Contemporary Cultures* (pp. 341–144). Cambridge MA: MIT Press.

Horton, D. (2006). *Social Movements and the Bicycle.* Paper presented to the conference, Alternative Futures and Popular Protest, Manchester Metropolitan University, UK, April 2006.

Horton, D. (2013). *Towards a Revolution in Cycling.* Retrieved from http://thinkingaboutcycling.wordpress.com/towards-a-revolution-in-cycling/ [accessed on 16 April 2013].

Horton, D., & Parkin, J. (2013). Conclusion: Towards a Revolution in Cycling. In J. Parkin (ed.), *Cycling and Sustainability* (pp. 303-325). Bingley, UK: Emerald Press.

Lenting, H. (2014). Comparing and Learning From Each Other for a Better Cycling Future. Paper presented to the Networked Urban Mobilities Conference 2014, Copenhagen 5/11/14.

McKay, G. (1996). *Senseless Acts of Beauty. Cultures of Resistance since the Sixties*. London, UK: Verso.

Melucci, A. (1996). *Challenging Codes: Collective Action in the Information Age*. Cambridge, UK: Cambridge University Press.

Miliband, R. (1984). *Class Power and State Power*. London, UK: Verso.

Mills, C.W. (1956). *The Power Elite*. Oxford, UK: Oxford University Press.

Mills, C.W. (1959). *The Sociological Imagination*. London, UK: Penguin.

Modood, T. (2013). *Multiculturalism: A Civic Ideal* (second edition). London, UK: Polity Press.

Mom, G. (2011). "Historians Bleed Too Much": Recent Trends in the State of the Art in Mobility History. In P. Norton, G. Mom, L. Millward & M. Flonneau (eds.). *Mobility in History: Review and Reflections* (pp. 15-30). Lausanne, Switzerland: Editions Alphil.

Mouffe, C. (1995). Feminism, Citizenship and Radical Democratic Politics. In L. Nicholson & S. Seidman (eds.), *Social Postmodernism* (pp. 315-331). Cambridge, UK: Cambridge University Press.

Nicholson, L., & Seidman, S. (eds.) (1995). *Social Postmodernism*. Cambridge, UK: Cambridge University Press.

Rosen, P. (2002). *Up the Vélorution: Appropriating the Bicycle and the Politics of Technology*. (SATSU Working paper N24 2002). Science & Technology Studies Unit, University of York, UK.

Shove, E., Pantzar, M., & Watson, M. (2012). *The Dynamics of Social Practice: Everyday Life and How it Changes.* London, UK: Sage.

Snow, D.A., Soule, S.A. & Kriesi, H. (eds.) (2004). *The Blackwell Companion to Social Movements.* Oxford, UK: Blackwell.

Stoeker, R. (1999). Are Academics Irrelevant? Roles for Scholars in Participatory Research. *American Behavioural Scientist,* 42(5), 840–854.

United Nations Convention on Road Traffic, Vienna, 8 November 1968. E/Conf.56/Rev.1/Amend.1 accessed at http://www.unece.org/fileadmin/DAM/trans/conventn/crt1968e.pdf.

Urry, J. (2007). *Mobilities.* Cambridge, UK: Polity Press.

Vivanco, L. (2013). *Reconsidering the Bicycle: An Anthropological Perspective on a New (Old) Thing.* London, UK: Routledge.

Williams, J.P. (2011). *Subcultural Theory: Traditions and Concepts.* London, UK: Polity Press.

Williams, R. (1976 [1983]). *Keywords: A Vocabulary of Culture and Society* (revised edition). New York: Oxford University Press.

Williams, R. (1985 [1958]). *Culture and Society 1780–1950.* London, UK: Penguin.

Wilson, D., with Papadopoulos, J. (2004). *Bicycling Science* (third edition). Cambridge, MA: MIT Press.

CHAPTER 2

DIVERSITY IN CYCLE POLICIES

Ida H. J. Sabelis

So many types of bicycles? That's only for the Netherlands; that would be impossible here!

In the Netherlands we have the ambiguous reputation of being a cycle-friendly country with nice infrastructure, well-trained car-drivers, and a multitude of policy instruments and conditions facilitating cycling for all. This may be so vis-à-vis some other (European) countries, but it does not automatically mean that we are a cyclists' paradise. Increasingly, a multitude of use(s), infrastructure and regulations show how we should abandon the idea of "cycling culture" as a singular notion. Indeed, cycles come in many forms, for different uses, and by different users. At the same time, this quality invites further investigation of use, habits and values concerning cycling. How has cycling increased over the last couple of decades? Has infrastructure adapted to the different users? Have politicians developed policies serving cycling as an instrument of sustainable mobility and transport?

This chapter emerges from a joint project by Peter van Bekkum, Maarten Heckman, Ida Sabelis and Maarten Sneep, carried out in 2010 and 2011 by the authors, and published (in Dutch) in the magazine of the NVHPV, the Dutch Association for Human Powered Vehicles (Recumbents), (van Bekkum et al. 2011; van Bekkum, 2012). The original study examined how cycling was presented in political programmes by various political parties in the Netherlands during the 2010 provincial (regional) elections. Through a case study, we demonstrated how, even within the policy context of the Netherlands, cycling cultures discursively and contextually differ, based on different views, assumptions and interests. This leads to insights in how cycling is considered important for different reasons. These reasons do not necessarily promote and support conditions for the expansion of cycling mobility. On the contrary, the discourses show how "cycling cultures" are presented as taken-for-granted, thereby limiting options for cycling rather than promoting new, coherent and diverse ways for (sustainable) mobility. The implication of the original study and its development in this chapter is that even where cycling is relatively well resourced, and has the status of an everyday activity and practical mode of transport, there remain gaps between existing policy and the kinds of thinking required for broader strategies of sustainable mobility. It provides insight on different levels. Practically, the examples show how different uses of cycling require increasingly different conditions (infrastructural, cultural, social and political). And on the theoretical level, the focus on cycling cultures in a small country may inspire cycling (social) theory in terms of interdisciplinarity, research methods and themes, and the further inquiry of cycling cultures as an important subfield of investigation.

Criticizing Paradise

How can we criticize cycling policies in a country that has a worldwide reputation as no less than a cyclists' paradise, and exports its knowledge and expertise across the globe? Members of the NVHVP both enjoy the benefits and meet the limitations of that paradise on a daily basis. Recumbent cycles place the rider feet-first in a seated position (as in a car) and have been produced since the 1930s (Cox & Van Der Walle, 2007), offering advantages of comfort and (potentially) speed. Where do all these riders travel, regardless of journey type, style of riding or choice of cycle? On cycling paths designed for standardized bicycles, with so many traffic lights, so few highway-like solutions for commuting cyclists, so many obstructions (poles, gates, barriers, etc.), and so many road users well trained to take notice of cyclists around every corner.

Many of us ride "Velomobiles", the teardrop-shaped or torpedo-like, covered tricycles measuring more than 2.85 m long, and 0.76 m wide, enjoyed for the weather protection, practicality and efficiency. And it could be argued that we are a pain to all other road users, cars and cycle lovers alike, for our speed, dissident road use, and sudden, relatively silent emergence. However, it can also be argued that the experience of such cyclists can be held representative for many other cyclists: where Velomobiles can pass, so can everybody else on two or more wheels, including riders of cargo bikes and those with trailers. Therefore, recumbent cyclists tend to view their experience as representative of the needs of (many) other diverse cyclists. The technical advantages of Velomobiles, trikes and other recumbents allow riders to regularly undertake longer distance journeys (as also do e-bikes), but at higher speeds for the same effort. Because of their intensive and frequent use of long-distance tracks, their collective experience exposes hitherto neglected needs for a range of riders and produces new ideas for cycling infrastructure, as well as providing a view on the multitude of cyclists all using the same paths. Moreover, "unusual" cyclists acknowledge the importance of developing a differentiated view on cycling from their growing familiarity with so many different cycle uses. Riders of recumbents and Velomobiles will almost always also be riders of other cycles as well.

Of course, leisure and tourist cycling requires different conditions, and so does sport cycling, riding for (and with) children, e-bikes, commuting, shopping, fast and slower cycling, carrying goods, flat, windy and mountain cycling, etc. If we want to take cycling mobility seriously in its full array, we should differentiate the different types and needs for cycling, per country as well as within countries, in order to shape diverse conditions for diverse uses as a gradual process (as argued in the previous chapter). Cycle paths are not the ultimate solution for all, nor are traffic lights (and the height of their controls, if user operated), bridges, fences and all other aspects of road design. Overarching policies to enhance cycling as a sustainable way of transport for short and medium distances should therefore be judged and evaluated for their capacity of promoting inclusiveness and differentiation. This means that we should strive for an understanding of cycling mobility as a diverse, layered and complex phenomenon, in which deviant appearance can be taken as another reason for adapting infrastructure, or cycle policies. Taking a deliberate stance on the margins, outside of the mainstream, provides a space for insight.

From the social sciences, we know that cultural diversity requires an approach in which we strive for participation of all (Cox, 1993; Janssens & Steyaart, 2001; Ghorashi & Sabelis, 2013), while at the same time allowing for diverse needs and solutions. One way to sharpen a diversity focus on cycling mobility is to look at existing programmes of political parties and of the occurrence and absence of nuance in cycle policies. A major concern of the evaluation is to ensure that policies do not deal with diversity by promoting competition between groups with disparate needs (for example, between fast and slow cyclists). Instead, solutions need to aim for inclusiveness to avoid fragmented solutions for mobility problems.

The analytical approach applied in this study transfers a model for "managing diversity" (Ghorashi & Sabelis, 2013; Zanoni et al., 2010), from management studies to issues of cycling, mobility and infrastructure. It is, therefore, a case study in transdisciplinarity. A core assumption in "managing diversity" is that through the process of introducing "others", that is, those outside of assumed norms, into an organization, unexpected solutions can emerge that benefit all (Ely & Thomas, 2001). Moreover, through developing diversity in terms of equality, it is often the case that policies are developed through which what was considered taken-for-granted is transformed into a pathway to new solutions. In such cases we can see how meeting the needs of a minority often leads to a majority benefit. To illustrate, where barriers for wheelchairs are removed, a lot of pedestrians benefit. But most importantly from a diversity perspective is the emancipatory quality embedded in a diversity approach: power relations and hegemonic regimes can be unmasked and replaced by more "democratic" insights and policies. This practice of applying the insights of one area of academic study to another specific area of social practice, in this case cycling, is increasingly important, and can lead to innovative and often unexpected insights (see for example Sabelis & van der Kloof, 2012)

Unravelling Dutch Cycling Culture

So the question remains. How can we investigate cycling culture in a country in which cycling is so taken for granted? As Horton et al. have argued, "The bicycle and cycling need *always and everywhere* to be understood in relation to the societies in which they exist" (2007, p. 7 – italics added by author). This chapter goes beyond this line of reasoning to attempt to both con-textualize the Dutch situation for cycling, and to present this situation as an inspiration for other contexts by critically looking at the downside of a "fixed" cycle culture. To put it another way, in a context where cycling is normal, habitual and unthought, what might be the negative dimensions of this situation? Lessons can be learned not simply by repetition of what exists, but understanding what the limitations of regular policy and practices are in situations of mass cycle use. To do this, we can gain a better perspective from assuming the stance of "others". We demonstrate that especially in the context of the Netherlands (and similar situations) it is important to unravel the taken-for-granted in order to gain an understanding of how cycling cultures (plural) can be established in different contexts,

47

allowing for mutual inspiration across societies in the dynamic development of cycling worldwide.

In the Netherlands, responsibility for developing and constructing cycle paths and other infrastructural conditions for cyclists lies with the Provinces (twelve, at the moment) and Communities. Roughly speaking, Provinces are responsible for inter-city cycling, and Communities for intra-city (or intra-village) use. In the course of 2010 the authors of the study considered how we could support the development of cycling policies by scrutinizing the plans of political parties on the topic of cycle friendliness. Fortunately, the Netherlands has a tradition of many parties participating in the elections, so that our investigation could compare a wide range of ideas, plans and visions. The programmes of ten nationally operating political parties (and some local parties) were read for the occurrence of "fiets" (bicycle). Then we looked for criteria for general cycle friendliness and more specifically for human powered mobility for a broader or more limited understanding of "cycling" in all its guises, and for all its users. So the task was not only to understand how cycling provision was to be achieved, but what sort of practices and users were envisioned by that term "cycling" in that context. To what extent was diversity comprehended as an issue? By using a discursive approach, we listed and highlighted passages of cycle friendliness and compared the descriptions used. Thus we could obtain validity by data saturation, and cross-validation through the comparative analysis of four interpreters (the four authors of the original study).

When the results of the discourse analysis were examined, particularly striking were the "extreme" results. These ranged from no mention of cycling policies at all, to (very) different suggestions, rates of interconnection and value estimation within individual parties across the Provinces. Apparently, for some parties, coordination of their cycling policies across the whole of the country remains an issue. In 2011 we followed up on our first investigation by again scrutinizing political plans, but this time by looking at what became of the plans after the provincial coalitions were formed. What was left of the election rhetoric? What had materialized into policies or plans, and what had not survived the political accommodation of coalition formation? This two-level analysis allowed us to interrogate not only the policy intentions and conceptualization, but also the salience of those ideas within the reality of political give and take.

In the first phase (election programmes), we scored plans and measures on a five–point scale ranging from positive to negative. The criteria for attribution as positive or negative were derived from the collective experiences of NVHPV members. So particularly positive scores were given for measures like cycle highways (ongoing routes); attention given to missing links in the (national) network of cycle routes; avoiding obstacles; the use of over or underpasses, green waves (i.e. traffic light coordination) in city areas; and most importantly, the overall coherence of plans. Negative scores were given, obviously, to plain absence of cycle policies and plans, or to one-sided and vaguely formulated measures like "the promotion of cycling" with no further specification. Most of these factors are present in broader lists of best practice in cycle promotion, but the particular stresses reflect the priorities of the "deviant" users.

All scores of all parties were included in an overall matrix (http://intercityfietser.nl/PS2011/ – Table 2.1 on p. 51) allowing an overview of parties per Province with a global estimate of cycle friendliness per party (Table 2.2 on p. 52). The matrix was linked to passages in the programmes and to the background information of the score. We could then formulate an evaluation of the political programmes, attribute a score per party, and formulate election advices per province. Additionally, in the follow-up investigation, we could trace what was left

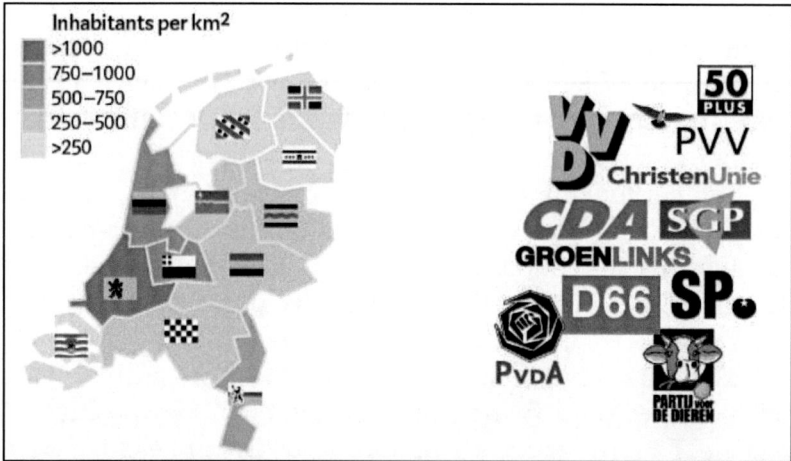

Figure 2.1: Population density for Provinces in the Netherlands and their political party logos.

of former plans, or how plans had materialized in the province plans (or not). The latter gave us, as a user-action group, information to confront, or praise, the parties with the outcome.

In evaluating the programmes, we distinguished between remarks about, or hints at commuters, or long–distance cyclists and "normal" cyclists, e.g. children, the everyday travel over short (neighbourhood) distances and for shopping. Cycle commuters generally cover longer distances, frequently at higher speeds and benefit from ongoing, obstacle-free routes. In the 2010 elections, we could see the emergence of e-bikes as a significant sector, and existing infrastructure is revealed as less than inclusive for all. More than recumbents or Velomobiles, e-bikes now raise the pressure to revise traditional infrastructure.

Provinces / Parties	VVD	PvdA	CDA	SP	GROENLINKS	D66	ChristenUnie	SGP	PVV		
Groningen	2	4	5	3	10	2	8	–	–	–	34
Friesland	3	–	1	3	19	–	2	–	–	–	28
Drenthe	–	3	18	–	3	10	–	8	–	–	42
Overijssel	4	3	8	–	7	3	5	5	–	–	35
Gelderland	0	7	10	9	16	7	12	7	–	–	68
Flevoland	1	–	2	–	7	–	5	–	–	–	15
Utrecht	1	12	–	11	24	24	12	6	–	–	90
Noord-Holland	6	5	2	4	12	17	3	15	–	–	67
Zuid-Holland	2	9	18	–	42	9	3	6	–	–	89
Zeeland	1	3	7	3	2	–	6	5	–	–	27
Noord-Brabant	7	2	7	6	8	3	5	5	–	–	43
Limburg	1	4	–	6	10	5	6	–	–	–	32
	28	52	78	45	162	80	67	57	–	–	

Table 2.1. Incidence of references to fiets (bicycle) in political manifestoes, by party and Province. *Source: Hans van Nieuwstraten.*

Provinces	Parties	VVD		PvdA		CDA		SP		GROEN LINKS		D66		ChristenUnie		SGP		PVV		50 PLUS		Regional parties	
Groningen		–	–	++	++	•	+	+	+	++	++	–	–	•	–			–	–	–	–		
Friesland		+	+	–	–	•	–	+	+	+	+	–	–	+	+			+	•	+	–		
Drenthe		–	–	–	–	++	–	•	•	++	++	++	+	++	•			–	–	–	–		
Overijssel		–	–	–	–	+	+	•	++	+	+	•	•	+	–			–	–	–	–		
Gelderland		•	•	++	++	+	++	•	++	++	++	++	•	+	+	++	++	–	–	–	–	+	+
Flevoland		–	–	–	–	+	+	–	–	+	+	–	–	+	+	+	+	–	–	–	–		
Utrecht		–	–	+	+	+	•	++	++	++	++	++	•	++	++	+	+	–	–	–	–		
Noord-Holland		–	–	+	+	•	+	+	+	++	++	++	++	•	++	++	++	•	•	–	–		
Zuid-Holland		–	–	++	+	+	+	+	+	++	–	++	++	•	–	++	++	•	•	–	–	+	+
Zeeland		•	•	++	++	•	+	•	•	+	+	–	+	+	+	+	+	•	•	–	–	+	–
Noord-Brabant		+	+	–	–	•	•	•	•	+	+	–	–	+	+	+	+	•	•	–	–		
Limburg		–	–	++	++	+	+	+	+	++	++	–	–	•	–			–	–	–	–	+	+

Table 2.2. Score sheet for cycle friendliness in the political programmes in relation to commuting long distances or everyday, shorter distance cycling, measured on a five-point scale as follows: ++ very positive, + positive, • neutral, – negative, – – very negative *Source: Hans van Nieuwstraten.*

Differences in speed become a problem on narrow cycle paths. And the more different users use the traditional infrastructure, the more new demands for alternatives emerge. In the Netherlands, "normal" cyclists are the millions of people who cover short/er distances, such as from home to school, for shopping and tourism purposes. Our original study did not pay specific attention to racer or sport cyclists, although we assumed that these cycle users should also benefit from measures as envisioned for commuters.

More specifically, the investigation made us aware how cycling is discursively constructed in different manners. Therefore, we took the opportunity in the context of "cycling cultures" to have a look at the discursive qualities, and specific modes of labelling "cycling" within the political programmes. Like the mythical "thirteen words for snow" attributed to the Inuit from Greenland, we expected a multitude of words for cycle conditions in a country like the Netherlands. For this purpose, we revisited the results of the 2010 and 2011 investigations and looked at the occurrence of words for cycling and contextual assumptions expressed in the material.

The results are graphically displayed in Figure 2.2 on p. 59. This representation reflects the occurrence of words and expressions related to cycling used in the texts studied, enhancing insights about cycling diversity, or all the diverse understanding of cycling hidden in the single term "fiets".

What is Under the Surface? (Results from the First Inquiry)
In many Dutch Provinces people have designed big plans to promote cycling, as evidenced by the 101 different plans studied (not all parties published their plans online or in time). We noted what we might call a competitive atmosphere: more than one Province prides itself in becoming "the no. 1 cycling Province of the Netherlands". Programmes on the provincial level build bridges between local and national interests. This implies that provincial themes appear in a set of political programmes of

parties, or that a specific point of interest will emerge in the programme of more than one party in a Province, often related to geographical and economic themes. At the same time, we may expect regional interests to appear in political programmes on the national level. So the question was raised, what would prevail: political issues or regional interests? Would we be able to pinpoint a distinctive national "sphere", or would local issues and needs be prominent? The available data is limited. It is a discursive study reliant on a published body of texts, which may in turn be shaped by (national) party political discipline and by desire to persuade an electorate. Nevertheless, we did find some fascinating patterns in and across the available data.

Across the available data from provincial programmes, some clear trends emerge. The use of cycle as in "cycle path" turns out to express specific styles of cycling use. The addition of "path" to "cycling" more than once is linked to leisure or to sport cycling. In some cases it is directly linked to tourism, expressed for instance by the addition of "shelter" and "relation to natural surroundings". Obviously, this is particularly valid for political parties from Provinces that benefit most from the economics of tourism. For instance, in Zuid-Limburg (south-eastern part of the Netherlands, bordering Belgium and Germany) and in Zeeland (Sea Land, the south-west, with a group of peninsulas and a formidable coast line) the orientation of political parties reveals a clear bias towards tourist cycling. In contrast, Utrecht and Zuid-Holland (central Provinces with a more than average level of cycle services) the orientation is towards commuting, via attention to long-distance cycling and commuting. So at provincial level, cycling in the Netherlands means different things in different places. Further, a tendency to either opt for, or promote cycling as an issue of sustainable transport can be discerned under the surface language. This differs from cycling with economics as the core perspective (commuting, tourism, accessibility). Only in some instances did we find a coherent view in which more than one element was linked to others (for example, economics to public transport; tourism to long-distance cycling; cycling more generally to sustainability and health). An example of coherence was found with the SGP – a Christian party – that in the Province of Drenthe presented plans in which it said:

> Mobility: focus on wider roads. It is desirable to create space both for public transport and for bicycles. Discourage use of cars. Strive for sustainable safety for vulnerable road users, e.g. cyclists. Investigate options for cycle highways in densely populated areas – no crossings with other traffic. More cycle parking with PT (Public Transport) stops. Tourism: invite entrepreneurs to develop market potential for long-distance walking, cycling and sailing. (http://www. sgp.nl)

An example of the relationship between cycling and sustainability is found with the Green Party (GroenLinks) in the Limburg Province:

> beyond traffic jams with bicycle, bus and train. In many instances cycling is the best alternative to car use. Cycling is a lot healthier as well. The Green Party would like to help everybody who now covers distances less than 10 km per car, to change to cycling. It will save time, and more importantly money. We don't have to remind you that cycling contributes in reducing CO_2 emission. To turn cycling into the alternative for driving cars, cycle paths have to be safe and convenient. So called cycle highways help you reach your destinations without crossing car loaded roads. You can unreservedly allow your children to cycle to school. (https://groenlinks.nl/)

Both political identity and local, or regional interest emerge in the political programmes. It still came as a surprise to our investigation how consistently the identity of political approaches could be linked to cycling values, that is, the relatively right wing liberals to economic issues, the Christian Democrats to leisure, and the Green Party to sustainability. It seems so obvious: the Green party has not left out cycling in any of the Provinces' plans. The new right-wing, or "one issue" parties leave out cycling altogether. And the liberal-conservative party links cycling to economics and commuting with growing attention to speed, expressed in attention to pedelecs (electric-assist bicycles limited to 24 km/h). The Christian Democrats in rural areas always take leisure and tourism for granted and thus promote cycle paths in "traditional style", e.g. expressed in terms of beauty, rest and enjoyment of nature. Cycling is evidently a politically laden term, with varying meanings, associations and connotations accorded by different ideological positions. But overall, we should acknowledge that all parties in the Netherlands, one way or another, at least mention cycling in their plans. We are fully aware that in other countries this attitude can be looked upon with envy. For the moment, however, we are just analysing the discursive use of "cycling" in electoral programmes here. The ultimate issue for the promotion of cycling diversity is what materializes, and how, through political action (plans/policies) after the elections.

Policies, Politics and the Status of Cycling (Results from the Second Inquiry)

Although one might expect otherwise, cycling does not emerge as a priority when it comes to building provincial government building in the Netherlands. This may be because cycling is so commonplace that not many people think of it as an issue. Even so, ongoing attention is needed to ensure it stays on the agenda. In harsh negotiations during the phase of coalition building following the election campaigns, other important issues (economics, natural resources) were balanced out against the relative unimportance given to cycling in a country of cyclists.

After the elections of spring 2011, coalitions were built and plans and programmes merged accordingly. In the process of coalition building, and with a specific financial context because of the international monetary crisis of 2008/9, the give–and–take of priority setting led to differences in cycling policies. In some Provinces, coalitions were built by three or four parties in which a majority originally presented cycling as an important issue and yet, after the elections, cycling somehow vanished from formal policy agreements. In general, the outcome was that in two Provinces in which cycling had most hits overall (see Table 2.2), the policies turned out to be very outspoken and coherent. Zuid-Holland and Utrecht, the two geographically most central Provinces (urban, with a service economy, densely populated) express a keen interest in long-term development of coherent (that is interconnected, serving more than one interest) and long-distance cycle solutions, sometimes well combined with public transport. From what was observed, the role and development of e-bike use is likely to become an important factor in the future, and further studies will be needed to explore the implications of these technologies, their uses and their interaction with existing cycling patterns. In Zeeland and Gelderland (south-west and middle-eastern part of the country) the outcome after the elections was rather disappointing for cycle planning: with no specific plans, or just some minor reference to tourist/leisure cycling. Gelderland in particular stood out negatively in this respect. With a coalition of three progressive parties combined with the liberals (the latter usually considered rather conservative in the political spectrum), this Province's outcome illustrates how cycling can vanish from agendas as soon as parties with no or little reference for cycling gain a majority.

It seems right, in the context of "nice plans" for which election programmes are famous, to present some inspiring ideas presented in the material which may become bigger issues in the future, or options that might deserve imitation elsewhere. First, the idea of rendering secondary roads specifically traffic-calm to make way for cycling and walking – sometimes this solution was a side-effect of communities planning through-roads – and just leaving the old roads "for all other traffic". Second, specific investments and attention for infrastructural projects across rivers and canals (or highways and other passages) provide unique opportunities to include cycle and walking paths. At the same time, they provide options that are never as expensive as similar solutions for cars, but are often considered inefficient. Finally, we found an elegant solution where firms promoted cycling by presenting "the good example": political bodies reimbursing travel fees per kilometre irrespective of whether car, bicycle or public transport is used.

Of course, these observations are not based on a strictly statistical analysis (as might be more common in sociolinguistic approaches to the same task. The focus of our inquiry was to consider how patterns in cycling policies develop. We did not pay attention to how cycling is balanced with other important political issues. This discursive analysis of cycling in pro-grammes, plans and policies-under-construction, does illustrate how cycling policies can come and, despite the rhetoric and public commitments, can disappear, and how interrelations fluctuate between economics, mobility, infrastructure and each party's political goal. As cyclists who conducted the original study, we are not complaining. After all, we do have cycling policies. Figure 2.2 illustrates our wealth in cycling culture: it can be seen as a discursive landscape picture of how policies are expressed in relative attention by political parties.

Nevertheless, undertaking this two-part study revealed how cycling policy, despite its apparent solidity, can become rather ephemeral in the political universe. Furthermore, we can begin to point towards a way of unpacking the unitary monolith of Dutch cycling. From the perspective of "deviant", unusual or just plain "other" cyclists in the context of normalized transport cycle use, we experience ways in which existing infrastructure in the Netherlands frequently does not suit all users simultaneously. Examining political manifestoes allows us to

Figure 2.2. Incidence of references to fiets (bicycle) in political manifestoes, by party and province.

Key: Dutch (English): Diabetes (diabetes); Fiets (bicycle); fietsforens (commuter bike); Fietspad (bicycle path); File (traffic jam); filebuster (traffic- jam- beater); fit (fit); gezond (healthy); humeur (mood); interlokaal (intercity); Investering (investment); ligfiets (recumbent bicycle); mobiliteit (mobility); obesitias (obesity); snelfietsroute (fast cycle route); stressreductie (stress reduction); velomobiel (velomobile); verkeer (traffic); woon-werk (commuting); ziekteverzuim (absenteeism).

explore not only how cycling policies can be framed to support existing (relatively high) levels of cycle use, but also to consider what changes might be required in the light of emerging sustainable transport agendas. If increasing cycle use implies an increasing diversity of uses and users, how does existing infrastructure, and existing policy, cope with these?

Conclusions

As mentioned previously, this study is based on the transference of the principles of "managing diversity" (Ghorashi & Sabelis, 2013; Zanoni et al., 2010) from one context to another, and examining the emancipatory implications for a broader public that providing for those not in the "normal" category has for a wider public. These assumptions provided the criteria for our evaluation categories. Applying these criteria revealed not just whether there was policy or what was planned, but enabled us to consider the implications of these kind of policies, and the assumptions behind them, for a range of different sorts of bicycle use. "General" diversity theory applied to cycling can be seen to enlarge existing norms and values. In other words, the idea that in situations of diversity, measures taken for "exceptions to the rule" usually produce more benefits for all: even unexpected ones. This line of thought was applied by explicitly taking the experience of "abnormal" cyclists such as recumbent or Velomobile drivers as a measure for judging the quality of policies. This leads, for instance, to the conclusion that providing for ongoing cycle traffic (cycle highways) results in benefits also for local cyclists, whereas the reversed line of reasoning has no such effect (short-distance conditions do not lead to benefits for long-distance cyclists, an understanding that is explicit in the *Cycling Route Plus Plans* of the Groningen Province).

Although probably a lot more can be developed from this approach, the combination of "diversity" and "cycling" applied to political programmes demonstrates diverse solutions: unravelling the assumptions about cycling leads to the need to be more precise about in which context which requirements are valid. When politicians discuss cycling and negotiate better conditions for cycling mobility and tourism – economic reasons lead to different styles of infrastructure than commuters' economics. Pinpointing diverse uses, especially via a discursive analysis of how people talk about cycling and cycling conditions, is a first step for change. As an example, we can see that providing solutions to meet the requirements of long-distance cyclists also helps short-distance cyclists, but that the reverse is not true. And finally, a happy cyclist is a cyclist who can safely, fast and comfortably reach his/her destination. It also really helps if car drivers are cyclists themselves.

References

Bekkum, P. van (2012). Ligfietsers in de Provinciale Politiek, *Ligfiets&*, 2012-2, 22-23. [Recumbent Cyclists in Province Politics – Twelve Province Coalition Agreements – with thanks to M. Sneep and M. Heckman].

Bekkum, P. van, Sabelis, I., & Heckman, M. (2011). Fietsen en Verkiezingen, *Ligfiets&*, 2011-1, 13-15 [Cycling and Elections – 101 Programmes for Provincial Elections revised].

Cox, P., & Van De Walle, F. (2007). Bicycles Don't Evolve: Velomobilies and the Modelling of Transport Technologies. In D. Horton, P. Rosen, & P. Cox (eds.), *Cycling and Society* (pp. 113-132). Aldershot, UK: Ashgate Publishing.

Cox, T. (1993). *Cultural Diversity in Organizations*. San Francisco, CA: Berret-Koehler Publishers.

Ely, R. J., & Thomas, D.A. (2001). Cultural Diversity at Work: The Effects of Diversity Perspectives on Work Group Processes and Outcomes. *Administrative Science Quarterly*, 46(2), 229-273.

Ghorashi, H., & Sabelis, I. (2013). Juggling Difference and Sameness. Rethinking Strategies for Diversity in Organizations. *Scandinavian Journal of Management*, 29(1), 78-86.

Ghorashi, H. & Wels, H. (2009). Beyond Complicity: A Plea for Engaged Ethnography. In S. Ybema, D. Yanow, H. Wels, & F. Kamsteeg (eds.), *Organizational Ethnography. Studying the Complexities of Everyday Organizational Life* (pp. 231-253). London: Sage.

Horton, D., Cox, P., & Rosen, P. (2007). Introduction, Cycling and Society. In D. Horton, P. Cox, & P. Rosen (eds.), *Cycling and Society* (pp. 1-24). Farnham, UK: Ashgate Publishing.

Janssens, M., & Steyaert, C. (2001). *Meerstemmigheid: Organiseren met Verschil*. Leuven, Netherlands: Leuven University Press.

Sabelis, I., & van der Kloof, A. (2012). Cycling Cultures. Upbeat to a Comparative Study of Human Scale Mobility. Paper Presentation at Velo-city Vancouver 2012, Scientists for Cycling meeting, June 2012.

Zanoni, P., Janssens, M., Benschop, Y., & Nkomo, S. (2010). Guest Editorial: Unpacking Diversity, Grasping Inequality: Rethinking Difference through Critical Perspectives. *Organization, 17*(1), 9–29.

CHAPTER 3

RHETORIC AND REALITY: UNDERSTANDING THE ENGLISH CYCLING SITUATION

Dave Horton and Tim Jones

Introduction

There is general consensus among policy makers that cycling for transport is desirable. But despite apparent efforts by successive governments over the last forty years to promote cycling the major trend is still towards *less* cycling for transport. In this chapter we examine the reasons for the apparent gulf between *rhetoric* of policy makers and the *actual* reality of cycling in England (Aldred, 2012). Drawing on evidence from a large-scale study on cycling in four English cities, we describe the reasons why only a minority of people cycle for transport. We then use this as our departure point to demonstrate how ideology works to restrict cycling and to encourage car use. By ideology we simply mean how any dominant culture develops ways of describing, explaining and justifying its own existence as an inevitable and natural way of life. The world – including language, concrete objects and action – is necessarily ideological, but dominant ideology tends so to saturate everyday life as to become taken-for-granted and invisible. To summarize, we argue that challenging the ideological foundations to people's current travel behaviour is *key* to encouraging more people to cycle.

Understanding Cycling in England

In England, and indeed the rest of the United Kingdom, cycling has become unusual. What just a little over half a century ago was a major mode of urban mobility has today become a very minor one. Cycling now accounts for around 2% of all journeys and 3% of commuter journeys (UK Department for Transport,

2010). And while current UK physical activity guidelines suggest that adults aged between 16 and 65 should be at least moderately active for 150 minutes per week (Public Health England, 2014), the evidence shows that cycling is becoming less significant for people in achieving this goal. For example, between 1995 and 2010 the average time spent cycling declined from 6 hours to 5 hours per person per annum (UK Department for Transport, 2011).

The analysis we present here to illustrate why the majority of people in England do *not* cycle comes from a large-scale UK Research Council funded study called *Understanding Walking and Cycling* which ran between 2008 and 2011. The study undertook a range of quantitative and qualitative research methods across four English cities (Lancaster, Leeds, Leicester and Worcester) to investigate ways in which households incorporate (or fail to incorporate) cycling and walking into routine everyday travel and the decision-making processes that lead to specific travel behaviour outcomes. The methods used included conducting a large-scale social survey of attitudes of the population to cycling and walking; spatial analysis of the built environment to investigate the association with self-reported travel behaviour obtained from the survey; in-depth interviews with a selection of householders probing attitudes to walking and cycling and the reasons why people chose particular modes of travel; mobile interviews with people whilst they made a routine journey by cycle or on foot to investigate journey experience; and finally, immersive ethnographic studies with a selection of participants to observe and understand the nature of everyday travel decision making – for more information about the approach and methods used see Pooley et al., 2013; Pooley, 2011. While our findings are specific to our case study cities, we are confident that they are relevant to most UK cities and indeed cities in most industrialized nations that are failing to tackle the car's widespread domination of urban space.

There are, of course, notable exceptions to this pattern. Some of these include established "cycling cities" such as Amsterdam (NL) and Copenhagen (DK) that, as the previous chapter demonstrates, are the inheritors of some forty years of planned interventions, both at city and national level. There are also noteworthy cities that are transitioning more rapidly to increased space for cycling and cycling modal share such as Munich (DE), Malmo (SE), Bordeaux (FR) and Seville (ES).

The Majority Who Do Not Cycle for Transport

The majority of people in the UK do not cycle at all – around two-thirds of the population reports cycling less than once a year or never (UK Department for Transport, 2011). Despite the low level of participation in cycling, findings from our large-scale survey revealed positive attitudes to cycling and agreement that cycling is good for saving money, reducing impact on the environment and for benefiting health. However, attitudes to cycling for transport were less strongly associated with enjoyment. Our more immersive qualitative research methods helped us to identify that it is often a combination of factors that made cycling for transport difficult and unpleasant for most people most of the time. Five main themes were identified that restrict the public's willingness to participate: concern about safety and risk; problems associated with the urban infrastructure; constraints imposed by families and lifestyles; the influence of culture and image; and the impact of weather and topography.

The most important reason why people in our study did not cycle was that they felt it is too dangerous to cycle under current circumstances. They were generally incredulous at the idea of cycling in city traffic and did not believe roads are sensible places to cycle because roads are dominated by large numbers of fast-moving motorized vehicles. Implicit in their responses was the underlying belief that roads are designed for motor vehicles and footways (pavements) are for pedestrians and there is little space left for cycling. Despite footway cycling generally being frowned upon, there was sympathy towards those that adopted this practice, particularly parents accompanying their children, given the alternative was often cycling on busy roads.

Most people who did not cycle did not own a bicycle but we found, where bicycles were owned, they were typically stored in garden sheds and were poorly maintained and lacked the equipment that makes functional cycling easier and a possibility for some journeys. This compounded the difficulty of even contemplating planning a journey by cycle as it would require extra effort compared to walking, or even jumping in the car, for short journeys.

The perceived difficulty of trying to move together by cycle as a family unit or multi-person household was more-or-less ubiquitous. Physical, psychological and emotional barriers of any one individual in the group can curtail the aspirations of other individuals in the group to conduct journeys by cycle.

The fact that cycling for transport was rarely practised also meant that it had never had the chance to gain a foothold and become a habitual and normal tool for short distance travel. Car use had become the default option for most people, because of the obvious ease and normality of using it, even for short journeys. Most people do not like to stand out as different and to adopt different norms of behaviour, and within a landscape dominated by car travel, to cycle for transport was seen as abnormal.

Although cycling is promoted by the UK government as a means of transport, we found that, in practice, people regard cycling as a means of leisure in much the same way as is the case in the USA (Jensen, 2007). The majority of people that we came across in our study that had at least some experience of cycling only cycled very rarely and did so primarily for recreation. This "perfect" and "acceptable" cycling takes place mostly in green and quiet space away from motor traffic and typically on a weekend when the weather is fine. More often than not these spaces are accessed by car and therefore, paradoxically, car use is induced by the desire to cycle in more desirable environs. The journey government most wants converted from car to bicycle, the peak-time commute, is exactly the kind of hectic and stressful cycling journey that most people are unwilling to contemplate. This suggests to us that if there is any hope of encouraging even "partial cyclists" to engage in utility journeys then more attention needs to be given to journey ambience so as to emulate the more relaxed and pleasurable experience of leisure cycling.

The Minority Who Do Cycle for Transport

Despite the low levels of cycling for transport in the UK, we spoke to people who represent the small proportion of the population for whom cycling is an important means of getting around. Our study revealed that these people form a tiny minority of committed cyclists who ride through choice and who have developed coping strategies to navigate difficult and dangerous cycling conditions. Many of these "hardened" cyclists tend to ride fast and assertively and wear cycling-specific gear. Their cycling often looked more like sport than an ordinary mode of urban transport. During the course of our research we came to understand that their identities and practices have been shaped in the process of "being a cyclist" so much so that some committed cyclists often struggled to understand why more people do not cycle, believing if they can do it, surely others can do it too. This was often evident during ethnographic interviews where personal stories about cycling often related to themes around tolerating the behaviour of some motorists and acclimatizing to current hostile urban cycling conditions to the extent that such conditions had become part of the "normal" practice of cycling. So, at the same time that the advantages of cycling are espoused by this group, it became clear that they inadvertently perpetuate their identity as part of a "cycling elite". We argue that this failure to recognize the accomplishment of riding in the city is one of the barriers to developing strategies that would bring about a more diverse landscape for cycling that does not demand the development of a strong cycling identity and willingness to "survive" the current transport system.

We also came across other people who ride out of necessity. Their cycling practices and experiences are quite different. Most of these "forced" cyclists often need to travel at unconventional hours or to places poorly served by public transport and would prefer, but cannot afford, to go by car. And whilst they acknowledged the benefits of cycling, their style of riding was distinct from that of the committed cyclists above. They tended to ride cheap bicycles and had little interest in or knowledge of how to effectively maintain them. They rode on footways to avoid busy roads because of anxiety about sharing space with motorized traffic. But implicit in verbal accounts of their cycling behaviour was an inferiority complex and deference to people travelling in cars. Underlying this was the perceived "legitimate entitlement", vis-à-vis use of road space, of cars over bicycles, which must not get in the way and hinder their progress.

What this shows is that there is a diversity of practice even within the small minority of people who do cycle for transport in the UK. But as we go on to highlight below, "cyclists" who negotiate the road system are often "homogenised", as somehow "abnormal", and moreover, as social deviants often in contempt of traffic laws.

"Inevitable" Mobility: Ideology and Culture

> To see what is in front of one's nose needs a
> constant struggle. (George Orwell)

To cycle in UK cities more often than not involves negotiating space shared with cars and larger motor vehicles. Few people are willing to do so, fewer still would contemplate negotiating large junctions that have been designed to facilitate the smooth passage of high volumes of motor traffic. Those who cycle must do so within a transport system stacked against them and which privileges travel by car. This ensures that to drive in the city is "normal" and to cycle is somehow "abnormal", even for short journeys where cycling would be the most sensible option. Cycling becomes marginalized and cyclists become a "nuisance", or worse, an object of contempt. Sections of the British media are complicit in peddling the image of cyclists as social deviants who have total disregard for traffic laws, some going as far as to suggest that cyclists "deserve to be decapitated" (see http://news.bbc.co.uk/1/hi/wales/north_east/7168530.stm).

The fact that many people do not even consider or contemplate cycling is inevitable within a transport system that has focused historically around ensuring safe passage and smooth flow of motor traffic. Car use is now the norm and is convenient and is considerably safer than half a century ago, whereas cycling has become more difficult and dangerous and therefore abnormal. UK mobility culture has been shaped by mass car ownership which in turn has shaped how the transport system has evolved under a paradigm that has fuelled faster and longer distance travel (Banister, 2008). Cycling has become less convenient, less comfortable, less safe and therefore less desirable. The normality of car use inhabits everyday consciousness, informing what people see and feel as ordinary and extraordinary, acceptable and unacceptable. Car driving becomes ever more attractive, cycling becomes ever less attractive. As driving becomes ever more ubiquitous, cycling becomes invisible. Cycling only gets noticed when its proponents agitate and momentarily break free from this ordinary repression. Out of their proper place (whether in the protest march or ride, in the figure of the jaywalker or the red-light jumper) cycling starts to become political, and a problem. By making visible an alternative ideology, they expose and fracture the dominant ideology of the car (Furness, 2007).

The problem extends beyond "mere" car ownership and use, to a more total structuring of life around the car, in ways hugely harmful to cycling. The car's domination is not simply over physical space, but just as profoundly over cognitive space. People's thoughts, values, identities, tastes and practices all become structured by and around the car (see also Urry, 2004). The world becomes seen through "car-centred eyes" and the cultural limits of imaging towns and cities uninhabited by cars. Or, as a group of protestors put it in 1972, "We believe we are fighting not only cars on the road, but cars in the head" (*Cycletouring*, October/November 1972, p. 150). The priority which motorized traffic has over people cycling (and walking) has become embedded in infrastructure, made routine, embedded spatially and culturally, and taken-for-granted to the point of seeming "natural". It is this priority that must be challenged if we want cycling to assume a more prominent role in the transport system. This is an ideological landscape which people live with and struggle to see, let alone articulate and critique. In his 1973 book *Tools for Conviviality*, Ivan Illich examined the car's monopolization of urban space. Illich notes how such a "monopoly is hard to get rid of when it has frozen not only the shape of the physical world but also the range of behaviour and of imagination" (1973, p. 55). In the years since Illich wrote those words, this monopolization process has spread and deepened. Across the world the car has continued to become the obvious and ordinary means of travelling even short distances. Whether or not people want to drive is irrelevant – driving simply becomes what people who have cars do. People who do not have a car of their own, but who have family or friends with cars, tend to be helped by those other people's cars. People without access to any car must get by as best they can: walk and/or cycle; use public transport and/or taxis; stay at home. The car-less are of course increasingly surrounded by, and their lives constrained by, other people's cars; and no doubt many of them dream of someday having a car of their own, and becoming "properly" mobile.

The car has colonized external and internal views; out of the window cars are everywhere, and our minds cannot imagine life without them. Over time people together produce cultures and these cultures feel durable and inevitable. Life has been built and has become ossified around the car. To the extent that car use has been structured into people's lives, cycling has been structured out. So, as we experienced in our study, talking with people about cycling always comes down to people trying to figure out how best cycling could *fit in with* the car-based world. Given this context it may seem impossible to consider the replacement of a car-based world with another based around more equitable and sustainable transport where cycling plays an important role. But as we noted earlier in this chapter, cities across Europe are beginning to depart from the idea that cars should have the unfettered right to the city and are progressively embedding cycling within a more plural transport system. Below we highlight the current impasse within UK mobility culture that is preventing the same patterns from emerging across English towns and cities.

Towards a Plural Mobility with Cycling at its Heart

> … we cannot expect shifts in practices to occur when only
> part of the choice architecture is altered, leaving much of the
> underlying basis for consumption practices unchanged.
> (Barr & Prillwitz, 2014)

Pro-cycling rhetoric by those in positions of power, from government to local municipal level, tends to mask the realities of continuing and much more powerful pro-car action. Where only small measures in favour of cycling are undertaken they in fact form a part of a much broader and deeper ongoing commitment to car ownership and use. The promotion of cycling is then merely a cosmetic gloss to things otherwise staying much the same. People are reluctant to cycle because they inhabit car culture; similarly, those who advocate cycling playing a more prominent role in UK mobility culture must recognize we too belong to a car culture which is unlikely to dissipate completely. As Paterson highlights, "Those arguing for transformations away from a car-dominated system, or even transformations within automobility, are often (not always) naïve about the way in which attachment to cars provides an important sustenance to a sense of self, autonomy and so on and thus ideological forces wanting to resist moves away from the car" (2007, p. 221).

In UK towns and cities, cycling schemes tend to be tacked onto a transport system in which the car's dominance goes unquestioned. In the social environment, a diversity of small-scale programmes and projects try to *nudge* people towards walking and cycling (Barr & Prillwitz, 2014), but these people live in a wider environment thoroughly structured by the car and drenched in pro-car messages. It is as if cycling's repression depends on its tokenistic promotion – this promotion hiding the facts of much more powerful processes working in the opposite direction. A striking illustration is provided by recent government policy: on 27 November 2014 the UK government announced £214m funding for cycling over a six-year period (equating to around £6 per head of population compared to around £20 in the Netherlands). Less than one week later, on 1 December 2014, it announced a £15 billion "roads revolution" for England.

Ideological analysis of the car's centrality to everyday life is not new (see for example: Dennis & Urry, 2009; Paterson, 2007; Kay, 1998; Illich, 1973) but it remains timely. Indeed, in an era which sees such positive rhetoric towards cycling, analysis of its continuing repression is especially necessary. Unless we think about ideology we fall into the trap of thinking that how people move around is largely up to them, a simple matter of choice. Recognizing the ideological foundations of culture prevents our falling into the trap of imagining people are in any way "free" to shift from driving to cycling. Ideology means people do what they must do, like what they must like, and resist what they must resist (Bourdieu, 1984). And for as long as sustainable mobilities are promoted in such naïve ways, they will stay marginal. It is naïve to ignore how culture mediates what we think people should do and what they actually do. Culture is always ideological, and mainstream culture embodies the ideology of the car, which means that culture forms on the whole a block to cycling mobility.

The current orthodox ideology makes car use normal and cycling mobility abnormal; its reversal requires radical action. As we have seen earlier, people with access to a car tend to travel by car and to cycle mainly for leisure. Those without access to a car tend to cycle mainly through necessity, but often begrudgingly – whilst dreaming of the car that would make life better. People's mobility practices – including their (dreams of) car use – are sensible responses to current physical and social conditions. To change them we must make other practices more obvious and sensible. For this we must make proper space for cycling in cities if we are to engage minds in imaging moving around by cycle and if we are to have any chance of "selling cycling" as a perfectly normal and expected way of moving around for short journeys.

The effective promotion of sustainable mobility, including cycling, requires the transformation of its opposite. This must be a political project because the current unsustainable paradigm needs contesting and replacing if sustainable mobility practices are not to be continually incorporated tokenistically around the edges of a transport system. And until unsustainable mobilities are actively contested, they will keep getting proposed as the best solution to common transport problems such as congestion ("more roads required") and pollution ("smarter, greener cars required"). The ideology of our car-based system is nowhere stronger than in the proposal of solutions (for example, see John Parkin and Glen Koorey's (2012) critique of the UK approach to cycle network planning and design).

Encouraging people to cycle, or cycle more within the current transport system, is not enough to build a thriving culture around cycling mobility. Transformation of that system away from a car-based one to a more plural one where cycling plays a more prominent role is challenging but quite possible – after all, the car's monopolization of society and space has occurred only over the last few generations. Indeed, recent developments in London demonstrate cycling is being taken more seriously by established political processes. Although there are broader economic, social, political and cultural changes making cycling more politically acceptable to the dominant culture (including the ongoing and globally competitive neo-liberal re-making of the car-based city under the guise of "liveability"), cycling's integration into political processes importantly follows sustained, high-profile and mass campaigns involving a broad range of institutions, including organizations such as *The Times* newspaper (see http://www.thetimes.co.uk/tto/public/cycle safety/), which would traditionally be regarded a core part of the dominant ideology, not an agent of change. We would suggest London is at precisely the point where re-making the city towards cycling is looking possible, even probable, and this is inevitably provoking a properly ideological conflict, with vested interests opposed to a reduction in the car's established "right to the city" (Walker, 2014). But let us be under no illusions, promoting cycling mobility is a political process; if promotion does not challenge the status quo, it is doomed to fail. This strategy means doing three things. First, encouraging people to see what they tend not to notice – the damage that moving around mainly by car is doing to our cities and to us. Second, reminding people that the way things are is neither durable nor inevitable and inspiring them with a better vision of how things could be otherwise. Third, accelerating the process of discouraging car use for short journeys in urban areas by making it less convenient and normal to drive and much easier (and therefore normal) to cycle.

Such a paradigm shift requires a *leap in ambition* amongst those in favour of cycling mobility. The necessary changes are big, comprehensive and systemic, and these changes need to be sold to people – including politicians – as not simply worthwhile but essential. The transition to a sustainable transport system where cycling plays a more prominent role requires a new physical and cognitive architecture of everyday mobility. Based upon our own research we have highlighted how people have come to accept and take-for-granted the domination of the car and to accept the marginalization of cycling. We have argued that the challenge is not simply about promoting transport choice (because we are not dealing with a level playing field) but is also about providing systems and developing structures which change the possibilities for action, variously constraining some actions and enabling others. Cycling has been oppressed by a car-based mobility system that has become naturalized. In the UK, this oppression needs wider recognition if an alternative culture of sustainable mobility is to flourish where cycling plays a more prominent role, rather than continuing to receive token support.

References

Aldred, R. (2012). Governing transport from Welfare State to Hollow State: The Case of Cycling in the UK. *Journal of Transport Policy, 23,* 95–102.

Banister, D. (2008). The Sustainable Mobility Paradigm, *Journal of Transport Policy, 15,* 73–80.

Barr, S., & Prillwitz, J. (2014). A Smarter Choice? Exploring the Behaviour Change Agenda for Environmentally Sustainable Mobility. *Environment and Planning C: Government and Policy, 32*, 1–19.

Bourdieu, P. (1984). *Distinction: A Social Critique of the Judgement of Taste.* Cambridge, MA: Harvard University Press.

Dennis, K., & Urry, J. (2009). *After the Car.* Cambridge, UK: Polity Press.

Department for Transport (DfT). (2011). *National Travel Survey 2010.* London, UK: DfT.

Furness, Z. (2007). Critical Mass, Urban Space and Vélomobility. *Mobilities, 2*, 299–319. doi: 10.1080/17450100701381607.

H.M. Government. (2014). *Moving More, Living More. The Physical Activity Olympic and Paralympic Legacy for the Nation.* London, UK: Cabinet Office.

Illich, I. (1973). *Tools for Conviviality.* London, UK: Calder & Boyars.

Jensen, O.B. (2007). Biking in the Land of the Car –Clashes of Mobility Cultures in the USA. Paper presented at Trafikdage, Aalborg University, Denmark, p. 23: http://vbn.aau.dk/files/16056852/ tdpaper133.pdf

Kay, J.H. (1998). *Asphalt Nation: How the Automobile Took Over America and How We Can Take it Back* (reprinted edition). Berkeley, CA: University of California Press.

Parkin, J., & Koorey, G. (2012). Network Planning and Infrastructure Design. In J. Parkin (ed.), *Cycling and Sustainability, Transport and Sustainability* (pp. 131–160). Bingley, UK: Emerald Group Publishing Limited.

Paterson, M. (2007). *Automobile Politics: Ecology and Cultural Political Economy.* Cambridge, UK: Cambridge University Press.

Pooley, C.G. (2011). *Understanding Walking and Cycling: Summary of Key Findings and Recommendations.* Lancaster, UK: Lancaster University.

Pooley, C.G., Jones, T., Tight, M., Horton, D., Scheldeman, G., Mullen, C., Jopson, A., & Strano, E. (2013). *Promoting Walking and Cycling: New Perspectives on Sustainable Travel.* Bristol, UK: Policy Press.

Public Health England. (2014). *Everybody Active, Every Day: An Evidence-Based Approach to Physical Activity.* https://www.gov.uk/government/uploads/system/uploads/attachment_data/file/374914/Framework_13.pdf

The Times (n.d) Cities Fit for Cycling. http://www.thetimes.co.uk/tto/public/cyclesafety/

Urry, J. (2004). The "System" of Automobility. *Theory, Culture and Society, 21,* 25–39. doi: 10.1177/0263276404046059.

Walker, P. (2014). The Opposition to London's Segregated Cycle Lanes is Living in the Past. *The Guardian.* http://www.theguardian.com/environment/bike-blog/2014/sep/16/segregated-cycle-superhighways-london-business-living-in-the-past [accessed 17 December 2014].

CHAPTER 4

LESSONS LEARNED THROUGH TRAINING IMMIGRANT WOMEN IN THE NETHERLANDS TO CYCLE

Angela van der Kloof

Introduction
As both a consultant and a cycling advocate, it is exciting to see the growing interest in cycling over the last five to ten years. Mayors of cities like Paris, Seville, Rome, London and New York talk cycling. A bookcase can be filled with books and magazines about cycling and bicycles feature in advertisements and shop windows. Dutch, Danish and German cities and towns have become best practice examples and websites and social media platforms celebrate bicycle infrastructure and people on bikes.

The pictures, stories and discussions arising about bicycle infrastructure in these countries tend to be pretty detailed (Garrard et al., 2008). Additionally, there is a lot of criticism and debate about which "solution" works and which one does not (Martens, 2013). This is a good thing: discussions clarify and sharpen the mind. Yet in contrast, I see little detail in the writing, talking and showcasing of cycling culture in the Netherlands. Nor is there proper analysis, critique or debate about the nature of our cycling culture. Traffic education, training of cyclists and motorists and specific cycling promotion events are mentioned, but rarely described, researched or analysed. Dutch government officials are invited to speak about cycling and it is regularly stated that "cycling is in our DNA", implying that cycling is something physiological. Consequently one could argue that it might be really hard for non-Dutch who want to promote cycling. This logic gives unwilling politicians, planners and engineers in other countries the perfect excuse not to invest in cycling. In her talk "Her Majesty's Bicycle" (original: *De Fiets van*

78

Hare Majesteit: Over Nationale Habitus en Sociologische Ver-gelijking) Giselinde Kuipers (2010) explained how the associations and backgrounds connected with cycling are for the most part irrelevant for the Dutch. Habits and uses around the bicycle are obvious, "You just take the bicycle. Everyone cycles. You would not know how to do it differently" (Kuipers, 2010, p. 8). In an attempt to help fill the gaps in knowledge of Dutch cycling culture, this chapter explores the phenomenon of bicycle lessons for immigrant and refugee women in the Netherlands.

Dutch Women on Bicycles

Typically, international articles, magazines, websites and literature appreciate the fact that in the Netherlands many women ride bicycles (Pickup, 1988; Garrard et al., 2012; Arora 2012). In *Making Cycling Irresistible,* John Pucher and Ralph Buehler explain that levels of cycling in the Netherlands, Denmark and Germany are not only high and growing, but that "cyclists comprise virtually all segments of society" (2008, p. 502). One of the facts with which they illustrate this, is that 55% of all bike trips in the Netherlands are made by women, compared to 28% of the trips in the UK and 24% in the USA. In between a set of numbers and graphs, a few words caught my attention: "cycling is gender-neutral in those three countries" (2008, p. 504).

This statement may be true for the term "gender" in the very narrow sense, only referring to a comparison of the average number of trips between males and females. But in a wider and more realistic perspective, gender refers to perceived differences between women and men and to the unequal power relations based on those perceived differences. In her article "Gender and Mobility: New Approaches for Informing Sustainability", Susan Hanson stresses that "mobility is not just about the individual …, but about the individual as embedded in, and interacting with, the household, family, community and larger society" (2010, p. 8). In her definition of gender she adds this perspective, in which the specifics of place, time and people are essential: "The processes that define gender are always inflected by other dimensions of perceived difference (e.g. age, ethnicity, physical ability) and develop through everyday practices in place, including of course practices relating to daily mobility" (Hanson, 2010, p. 8).

The notion of gender roles in society, connected with factors such as age and ethnicity helps us understand travel patterns and mode choices better (Hajinikitas, 2001; Lehner-Lierz, 2003; Greico, 2006; Bonham & Wilson, 2012). By looking deeper into the Dutch case from this non-infrastructural perspective it becomes clear that it is much more accurate to say that cycling infrastructure is gender neutral in the Netherlands. The use and image of the bicycle are not.

Differences in Bicycle Use

In societies where it is mostly women who are responsible for running the household and for care for children and the elderly, improvement of the accessibility of shops, schools and health care services by bicycle is an important measure to increase cycling levels amongst women. At the same time, it is often overlooked that the same gender roles also influence women's opinion and concerns about safety in traffic. Women are not just concerned for their own potential to be injured or killed, but they also fear the consequences for daily life in their family in the case of an accident. As it is their responsibility to bring the children to school, for example, they will also take the child's perspective into account when thinking about safety en route. The following examples will illustrate that cycling is not gender-neutral in the Netherlands once we take factors like age, educational level, region and urban density into account and that gender roles matter even in countries with safe infrastructure.

According to the Centraal Bureau voor de Statistiek (2012), from which all the following figures are drawn, the average bicycle travel time per person, per day in the Netherlands is 12.96 minutes. In Table 4.1 we can see that 15- to 25-year-old males in the south of the Netherlands and 15- to 24-year-old females in the north of the Netherlands have a bicycle travel time of over 24 minutes a day, almost twice as much as the average. In contrast, 25- to 45-year-old males in the north and in the south of the country spend less than 8 minutes per day on the bicycle, which is almost as low as 65+ females in the west and the south of the country who spend 7.68 minutes per day on cycling.

Table 4.1. Bicycle travel time per person, per day according to age, gender and region (in minutes).

		0-15 years	15-25 years	25-45 years	45-65 years	65+ years	Total
Males	North	20.65	21.84	7.84	11.47	14.47	13.79
	East	18.64	17.49	8.00	11.52	13.52	13.03
	West	15.67	18.13	12.27	12.17	13.20	13.72
	South	19.33	24.71	7.67	10.25	11.12	13.07
Females	North	18.01	24.94	12.63	11.78	8.66	14.08
	East	16.50	21.12	9.08	11.93	9.49	12.72
	West	15.09	15.25	11.96	13.39	8.19	12.63
	South	13.63	15.69	10.25	11.16	7.68	11.16

If we look at the number of bicycle trips per person per day (Table 4.2), it is striking that in the 12- to 18-year-old age groups, both males and females have about 1.5 bicycle trips a day, whereas no other group older than 18 reaches even one trip a day. This supports the idea that for youngsters in the Netherlands cycling is a crucial way to get around independently. Of all adults, the 30-40 year old females come closest with an average of 0.87 bicycle trips a day. Men in the same age group have only 0.54 bicycle trips a day.

Table 4.2. Number of bicycle trips per person, per day according to age and gender.

	Males	**Females**	**Males and females**
All ages	0.68	0.80	0.74
0-12 years	0.96	0.92	0.94
12-15 years	1.67	1.59	1.63
15-18 years	1.54	1.43	1.48
18-20 years	0.87	0.73	0.80
20-25 years	0.60	0.71	0.66
25-30 years	0.54	0.72	0.63
30-40 years	0.54	0.87	0.71
40-50 years	0.51	0.81	0.66
50-60 years	0.52	0.78	0.65
60-65 years	0.58	0.81	0.69
65-75 years	0.58	0.64	0.61
75+ years	0.47	0.25	0.34

Education also influences bicycle use in the Netherlands, especially when examined in combination with gender. Table 4.3 shows that the lowest bicycle travel times per day can be found amongst males and females of average educational levels. The highest bicycle travel times can be found amongst males with low educational qualifications and females with high educational qualifications.

Table 4.3. Bicycle travel time per person, per day according to gender and education (in minutes).

	Males	Females	Males and Females
Younger than 12	12.78	11.08	11.95
Low education	14.78	11.67	13.04
Average education	10.82	10.96	10.89
Higher education	13.01	13.40	13.20
All categories	13.44	12.48	12.96

Table 4.4 gives figures for number of bicycle trips in the same categories as Table 4. The Dutch average is 0.74 bicycle trips per day.

Table 4.4. Number of bicycle trips per person, per day according to gender and education.

	Males	Females	Males and Females
Younger than 12	0.96	0.92	0.94
Low education	0.62	0.65	0.64
Average education	0.56	0.73	0.64
Higher education	0.63	0.93	0.77
All categories	0.68	0.80	0.74

The groups that contribute most to this high average figure are boys and girls up to 12 years old and women of higher educational levels. These three groups score between 0.92 and 0.96, almost one bicycle trip a day on average. The lowest levels can be found amongst all males above 12 years old (between 0.56 and 0.63) and women with low educational levels (0.65).

Actually, it is only females of average education who score around the average.

Combining Tables 4.3 and 4.4, we see that lower educated males have a low number of bicycle trips per day, but those account for the highest number of minutes on the bicycle per day. The males with higher educational levels also have a low number of trips and an almost average time spend on the bicycle. Males of average educational levels combine the lowest number of trips on the bicycle with the lowest number of minutes on the bicycle. The females with higher educational levels combine second highest numbers of trips with the second highest time spent on the bicycle. They spend almost as many minutes on the bike as men of lower educational levels, but need more trips for it.

The last table to illustrate that cycling in the Netherlands is not gender-neutral shows time spent travelling by bicycle correlated with country of birth and urban density of Dutch residence, further broken down by gender (Table 4.5 on page 86).

Again, the starting point is that average bicycle travel time per person, per day in the Netherlands is 12.96 minutes. When we look at the total for all males, they cycle about a minute a day more compared to females: not a big difference. But when we look further we do see some interesting variations. Comparing different urban densities and gender for the category "both parents born in the Netherlands", the highest amounts can be found in very urban environments. Both males and females cycle almost 15 minutes a day. The lowest are the males and females in areas of little urbanization, cycling about 12 minutes a day, making a difference of about 3 minutes between the highest and the lowest amounts. For the "Origin in western country" category the difference increases to 5 minutes a day between the group with the most minutes of cycling a day (the males and females in very urban environments at 13.6 minutes a day) and the ones with fewest minutes of cycling a day (females in a non-urban environment).

Lastly, in the category "Origin in non-western country" there is a difference of almost 10 minutes a day. These males in the urban environment spend as much as 19 minutes a day on the bicycle and these females in the very urban and urban environment as little as 9 minutes a day. Of all groups in this table, the males originating from a non-western country, living in an urban environment, spend most time on the bicycle. Compared to native Dutch males and females about 5.5 minutes a day more. And females originating from a western country and living in a non-urban environment spend the least number of minutes on the bicycle; a little less than the females of non-western origin.

The figures confirm that factors like age, educational level, region, urban density and country of origin matter significantly when we look at bicycle use. If the choice to ride a bicycle were purely based on availability of safe, convenient and attractive infrastructure, then the cycling rates for native Dutch women, and those with a different origin living in the same type of environment, would be equal.[1]

---

[1] Note that in Table 4.5 there are no separate figures for males and females of non-western origin available, so these are left out of the comparison. Numbers for the category "time spent travelling by bicycle correlated with country of birth and urban density of Dutch residence, further broken down by gender" are insufficient to be statistically viable.

Table 4.5. Bicycle travel time per person, per day according to gender, country of birth and level of urbanization (in minutes).

MALES AND FEMALES	Nether-lands	Very urban	Urban	Mode-rately urban	Little urban-ized	Non-urban
Combined	12.96	13.13	13.16	13.61	12.19	12.55
Both parents born in the Netherlands	13.36	14.61	13.23	14.16	12.32	12.83
Origin in western country	11.35	13.6	11.48	10.19	9.59	9.77
Origin in non-western country	11.51	9.36	14.04	11.43	13.80	9.65
MALES						
Combined	13.44	13.25	13.83	13.99	12.78	13.18
Both parents born in the Netherlands	13.59	14.59	12.98	14.51	12.98	13.38
Origin in western country	12.28	13.65	13.15	11.35	9.99	10.69
Origin in non-western country	13.30	9.79	18.97	11.08	12.63	–
FEMALES						
Combined	12.48	13.01	12.50	13.24	11.60	11.92
Both parents born in the Netherlands	13.12	14.63	13.47	13.81	11.66	12.29
Origin in western country	10.51	13.56	9.83	9.27	9.27	8.71
Origin in non-western country	9.72	8.96	9.10	11.80	15.07	–

HALIMA (± 1954)

"I learned to cycle, speak Dutch and cook, and I have tried to gain my place here, but I am still a stranger."

(arrived in the Netherlands in 1973,
raised in Casablanca, Morocco)

In that period I had good contacts with another neighbour, Mrs Prins. She often shouted out of the window: "Hé, Halima! Stop what you're doing and come outside with the children!" She taught me to bicycle. At first I practised on the street, but people were staring at me too much, I did not want that any more. I took my children to a meadow nearby and that is how I learned to cycle. By falling and getting up again. Once I could do that Mrs Prins suggested to make long cycling tours, along farms and meadows. In the beginning I was ashamed as I was swinging on the road, but Mrs Prins said: "You should not worry about that!", and that is what I did. It was wonderful. One day she said: "Tomorrow we will take the bicycle into the city!" I was shocked. The city was far too chaotic for me. Mrs Prins calmed me: "You have to try it once or twice, and the fear will disappear." I had nightmares about traffic accidents and once we started to ride I was afraid I would not make it alive. A truck rode behind me. I was so scared, I got stuffy, but I said to myself: "Persist, Halima!" Since then I was bold enough to cycle past buses and cars. Soon after I went everywhere by bicycle.

Author's Translation from Dutch, original in Hanina Ajarai & Marjolijn van Heemstra, "Land van Werk en Honing; Verhalen van Marokkaanse Moeders Over Hun Migratie", Bulaaq, 2006, pp. 122, 133, 134.

Box 4.1. Halima's experience.

A Journey Towards Understanding the Teaching of Cycling

For native Dutch people it is hard to imagine what it is like *not* being able to ride a bicycle. Still, one of the factors explaining the differences in bicycle use between women of diverse origin who all live in the Netherlands, is the fact that not all adults have the skills necessary to be able to cycle in traffic. Especially not when children need to be taken on the bicycle or have to be cared for by someone else whilst you are going to your activities. This is brilliantly illustrated by the story [Box 4.1 on p. 87] told in 2006 by a Moroccan mother who migrated to the Netherlands in 1973.

Not all women were lucky enough to have a neighbouring Mrs Prins and cycling lessons have been offered in women's centres, community centres and education centres for adults from the 1970s onwards. In fact, it was those women themselves who expressed an interest in cycling and identified the need to learn this in small groups in a somewhat protected environment (van der Kloof, 2003). At first mainly women from the Mediterranean and from Surinam joined the lessons as those were the countries of origin of most immigrants. Over the years, refugee women and, to a lesser extent, female expats started to join the courses.

I became involved in organized bicycle lessons in spring 1991 when the Centre for Immigrant Women in Tilburg (Netherlands) recruited volunteers to teach women to ride bicycles. This was the start of my personal journey to teach women from all over the world to make the bicycle a new part of their daily lives. Being a student in my early twenties, having been brought up with the bicycle, did not necessarily mean that I would be good at teaching adults from all over the world to cycle, though. In their book *Telling Ain't Training*, Stolovitch and Keeps (2002) explain how an expert is not automatically a good trainer.

> You would think that if each of these SMEs (subject matter expert) knows so much, they should have no trouble making the other person learn. But it's not happening because experts and novices do not process information in the same way. In fact, the greater the expertise, the less the expert thinks like a novice learner." (2002, p. 31)

Looking back at it, I think the situation was even worse, as I – a typical Dutch person who rides a bicycle every day – did not see myself as an expert. Cycling was something I just did, a second nature, and I had no idea exactly how I learned it as a child, let alone how to teach an adult. At that (pre-World Wide Web) time, we had hardly any training materials, apart from a few old bicycles, and we had no documented teaching method. As it turned out, this was pioneering work in which I was able to combine my passion for teaching and learning, with stimulating and supporting women from all over the world to overcome all sorts of barriers to cycling. For several years it became my personal journey to figure out good quality and fun methods, materials and an organizational system in which adult women could be taught the ability to ride our streets (van der Kloof, 2009).

The first thing we as cycling teachers had to do, was to become conscious of the fact that we were *unconsciously competent* in cycling for daily transport. Back in 1950 Maslow described his famous four stages of learning, as shown in Figure 4.1.

	Incompetence	Competence
Conscious	2 – CONSCIOUS INCOMPETENCE	3 – CONSCIOUS COMPETENCE
Unconscious	1 – UNCONSCIOUS INCOMPETENCE	4 – UNCONSCIOUS COMPETENCE

Figure 4.1. Maslow's four stages of learning.

At stage one, someone is not conscious of what they do not know. For example, someone who comes from a village in the mountains where nobody uses the bicycle might not be conscious of the fact that he/she does not know how to ride it.

The beginners in the cycling courses can be located in stage two. They are aware that they do not know how to ride the bicycle. During the course they learn the ability to ride, leading to stage three. After they have been riding for a while, the required movements become second nature and they no longer have to think about it consciously. In other words, they have reached stage four. Teachers and trainers should transcend the fourth phase and be conscious of their unconscious competences in order to understand what their abilities are, what they know and how that fits into the specific context. It will help them when attempting to transfer skills and knowledge to others.

In knowledge management, the term "tacit knowledge" is used to talk about this kind of unconscious knowledge. It is difficult to explain this knowledge to others, in comparison with explicit knowledge. The term was introduced in philosophy by Michael Polanyi who stated that "we know more than we can tell" (1966, p. 4) and interestingly enough his most famous example of tacit knowledge is the ability to ride a bicycle.

> If I know how to ride a bicycle ..., this does not mean that I can tell how I manage to keep my balance on a bicycle ... I may not have the slightest idea of how I do this, or even an entirely wrong or grossly imperfect idea of it, and yet go on cycling ... merrily. Nor can it be said that I know how to bicycle ... and yet do not know how to co-ordinate the complex pattern of muscular acts by which I do my cycling. ... I both know how to carry out (this performance) as a whole and also know how to carry out the elementary acts which constitute (it), although I cannot tell what these acts are. (1966, p. 4)

We often take this knowledge for granted and it can only be transferred "through practice in a particular context and transmitted through social networks" (Schmidt & Hunter, 1993). It requires personal contact, regular interaction and trust to transfer this knowledge: a very relevant observation when thinking about teaching an adult to ride a bicycle.

Materials and Methods

In the Centre for Immigrant Women in Tilburg, learning to cycle was not seen as an aim in itself. To us, cycling was a means of integration and emancipation for women who took the lessons. We saw that the ability to use the bicycle helped them to:

- adapt to the local usages and modes of transportation;
- broaden their mobility;
- enhance their sense of equality;
- enhance their sense of freedom.

Therefore it is clear that cycling is a tool for more equal participation in Dutch society (van der Kloof, 2013). And if the process of learning to ride a bicycle is to contribute to participation and emancipation, more than just teaching the mechanics of bicycling is required (Wolters, 2011). The learners were the starting point in all the materials developed, both in the materials for learning the rules of traffic for cyclists (see van der Kloof, 1996) and in the materials offering a teaching method for practical cycling skills (see van der Kloof, 2002).

Groups of learners are usually very diverse in age (from 15 to 60), educational level (from illiterate to professor), daily occupation (usually a mix of housewives and working women), having children or not, socio-economic background and experiences in traffic and public space in general. Typically, a teacher is assisted by one or two volunteers to teach a group of six to twelve women.

Some of the starting points for the teaching method for practical cycling skills are that:

- Learning the movements of cycling can be done in tiny steps. Each tiny new step is worth applauding and boosts self esteem.
- The learner has to learn herself: by watching, listening, trying and making mistakes. There is no need to hold the learner back.
- Each person has a preferred learning style and pace. Trainers must adapt to the personal style of the learner.

Fear is the number one constraint in learning to ride a bicycle. There are the obvious fears, such as falling, damaging a car or being hit by a car. But there are also fears of the consequences of an accident. Who will do the cooking, washing and bring the children to school if you break your leg?

The materials that we developed to support the learning of traffic rules for cyclists are based on the following:

- The image is the most important feature in communicating the core message. The text only supports the image.
- All images have a cyclist with a yellow jacket as a reference point.
- Explanations of traffic regulations should be made straightforward and clear; one rule at a time and starting at the most basic level.
- The text is written as a series of short, active instructions, dealing with concrete actions that suit the situation on the image. For example: "Cycle on the right side of the road" and "The traffic light is red. You must stop."

All materials and methods have been developed while working with colleagues and participants in the courses, and learning from experiences elsewhere. The open and collaborative approach enabled us to create an atmosphere in which it was possible to talk about what made it fun to learn to cycle as an adult, what constraints were being faced and find out how we could give support to overcome these barriers.

Teaching New Skills, Meeting Unknown Constraints

> *I thought that learning to ride a bicycle was too late for me.*
>
> Leïla Schraa
>
> Former participant in bicycle lessons, who became a cycling teacher.

Box 4.2. Leïla's experience.

An interesting concept that helps categorize and understand what exactly needs to be learned and which constraints might pop up when adults start to learn to ride a bicycle is the term "motility" introduced by Kaufmann et al. (2004). They define motility as the capacity of persons, goods and information to be mobile in social and geographic space. In other words, the potential mobility a person has, given who they are and where they are. Motility recognizes that actual or potential mobility may be realized differently or have different consequences across varying socio-cultural contexts. A person's motility consists of three elements, illustrated by Figure 4.2. *Access* refers to mobility options in time and place, the actual options and conditions in the specific socio-cultural context. Examples are access to a means of transportation like public transport, a car or a bicycle. *Competence* includes skills and abilities that enable a person to make use of particular transportation means. The last element is *appropriation*, which refers to how individuals, groups, networks or institutions interpret and act upon perceived or real access and skills. It relates to values and motives and describes how specific options are considered, deemed appropriate and either selected, or not. In Figure 4.2 the elements of the motility of a person are shown in relationship to the person's tacit knowledge and environment.

The following sections will explore the three elements, access, competence and appropriation in reverse order, because when we talk about women and cycling, appropriation dominates the other dimensions.

Appropriation is about values, motives and actual behaviour and is strongly linked with gender roles, age, ethnicity and regional differences. Motives expressed by non-native Dutch women for learning to ride a bicycle are, typically: to gain or regain quick and easy independent mobility; peer pressure; and health reasons. Other motives that have been mentioned are that one's children can cycle and a consequent desire to be able to

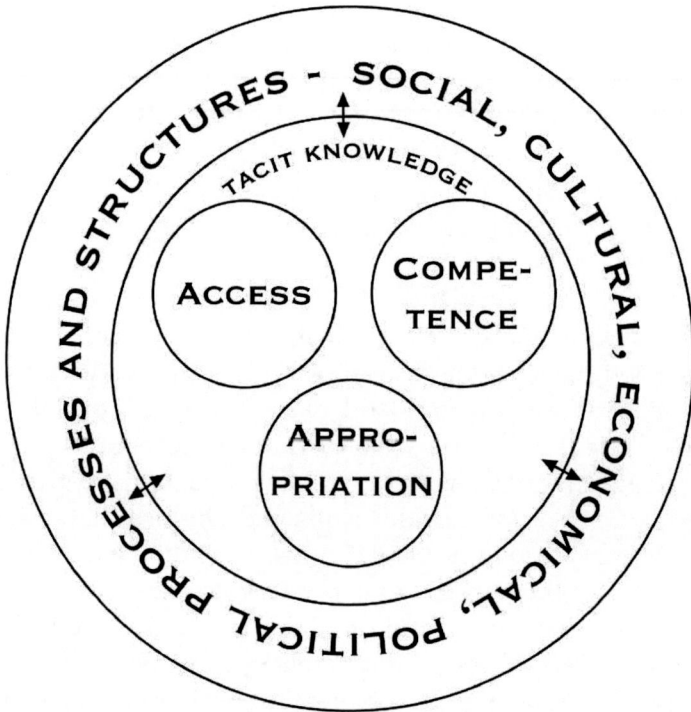

Figure 4.2. A person's motility in relation to tacit knowledge and the environment.

ride with them, and a wish to adapt to local mobility habits. These motives derive from what men and women see in daily life in the Netherlands. Cycling is not the same thing as it was in their country of origin. It is safe and convenient. Men and women, young and old are seen on the bicycle every day. Bicycles feature in product advertising, in movies and books. The value given to the bicycle in the new homeland differs from that of the country of origin and habits are completely different. To see women on bicycles, to realize that they are proper women and nothing harmful happens to them through riding is a strong message. It becomes even more so as increasingly diverse people on bikes are seen, including, for example, women who wear visibly Muslim clothing. This does not automatically mean that it is easy or quick to overcome cultural barriers.

Time, support, practice and a lot of perseverance are necessary when you've always been told that cycling is not a proper activity for girls and women, that women should wear dresses and these are not suitable for cycling and that you should not look people in the eye. Capacity is linked with confidence, self-esteem and the image of oneself and others (van der Kloof et al., 2014).

As a specific example of these processes, I clearly remember one Turkish participant of a training course, in her forties. It took her quite a while to learn to balance, but finally she was confident enough and I cycled with her in quiet streets, which went perfectly. For the next four weeks she could not come to the lessons as she was on pilgrimage to Mecca; no problem. When she returned we had a long conversation in which a Turkish colleague participated as well. The woman explained that she had asked a religious advisor in Mecca whether it was proper for women to cycle, as she was not completely comfortable with it. She was looking for support. The advisor told her that it is better when women do not cycle; but for emergencies she could use the bicycle. My first reaction was disappointment; why had I given my time and energy to support her in learning to ride when she was so easily taken off the bicycle again by a religious advisor? My colleague, however, started to ask more questions and it became clear that the woman had no intention to quit cycling. She had thought about it a lot and said: "I do not live very far from my daughter, but it takes a lot of time to go there on foot. I often need to go there and for those emergencies I am allowed to cycle." This experience opened my eyes!

Many myths surround cycling in some social groups and these are also part of the (non-)appropriation. Some of the most frequently heard myths around cycling are "it is improper for girls and women", "it is too difficult for women to learn" and "it is only for sporty and very healthy people". These ideas have also circulated in western European societies since the nineteenth century. Especially (but not only) for women, uncertainty about the body and appearance in public space plays a role. This is often true for discussions around arriving at work being sweaty, wearing the wrong shoes or having a problem with hairstyle. Apart from that, people just do not want to stand out from the norms of the group and do not want to be laughed at. When the norm is not to cycle, you need time, support, practice and a lot of perseverance to make a real change happen.

A highly relevant last aspect of appropriation is that it is shaped by needs, plans, aspirations and understandings of individuals, groups, networks and institutions. In many families, it is not routine to ask each member what their personal needs, plans and aspirations are, or how they understand the world. When you are a member of a group with a collectivist orientation (as compared to an individualist orientation) your actual personal behaviour is shaped not only, or not at all, by your own needs, plans, aspirations and understandings. Instead, it serves the needs, plans, aspirations and understandings of the group. This leads to an attitude in which women are used to letting priorities of others prevail. For example, this may result in a situation in which the woman in the household does not have a strong say over finances. Therefore, the need to buy a suitable bicycle is overruled by other priorities in the family. Similarly, if a family member drops by, exactly at the time of the bicycle lesson, hospitality will prevail over the personal need to learn to ride.

Competence is about the physical ability to move and the skills acquired. Within this we also have to understand the place of licences, permits, rules and regulations of movement that shape mobility on a structural level, as well as the personal knowledge required for wayfinding. Learning the very basic requirement for cycling may seem even too simple for the experienced rider. The first stage of competence is not to ride but to walk with the bicycle and to make sure we can do it without bruising our shins black and blue through hitting the pedals. Only then can balance and other basic skills be learned and practised. After acquiring those skills, it is time to practise riding in traffic. Some participants have hardly any experience in traffic and they have no experience with the speed of the bicycle and handling the vehicle.

Another field of competence is knowledge of the rules of the road for cyclists. The rules of the road in the countries where many of the participants come from, such as Morocco, Turkey, Iraq or countries in West Africa are very different from the rules in the Netherlands. Beyond the formal regulations lie unwritten rules: something even more difficult to teach. Wayfinding in your neighbourhood and beyond is an important competence when learning to ride a bicycle and starting to use it in your daily life. It is not self-evident that everybody has those competences. A substantial number of the participants have been in school for only a couple of years; some are illiterate, causing more than a lack of language competences. A typical constraint for some women is that they are not used to going to places on their own, and have not developed the wayfinding and navigational skills that come through experience.

Organizational skills are also important competences, but are easily overlooked. Kaufmann et al. (2004) talks, for example, about planning and synchronizing activities. Adults who start a course need to plan around their existing daily pattern. For women with a job, with younger children, or with many children, this can be a substantial barrier, as, for example, childcare needs to be arranged. Once able to cycle, you then have to figure out and organize how to take the children with you on the bicycle or next to you. The last competences that should be considered are the knowledge and skills around the mechanics of the bicycle. Most women starting out lack the knowledge and skills to repair flat tyres and bike lights, not to mention more complicated technical issues that can arise when starting to use the bicycle for daily transportation (see Cox, "Women, Gendered Roles, Domesticity and Cycling in Britain, 1930–1980" in this volume for a historical perspective on these competences).

Access refers to the options in time and place. In this case it refers to the availability of a bicycle, to services and to equipment. It is not just any bicycle that should be available; a comfortable bike to learn on and to use while you do not feel sufficiently safe must allow the rider to rest both feet on the ground at any given time. So the saddle should be low enough and the frame not too high. Unfortunately, with an average height of 1.68 m Dutch women are amongst the tallest women in the world, compared to women from Italy (1.65), Turkey (1.62), Brazil (1.59), India (1.52) and the Philippines (1.50). These few centimetres matter a lot. Dutch standard sizes for bicycles are too large (not only for beginners), making it more difficult and more expensive to find a suitable bicycle. Smaller frame bicycles rarely appear second hand.

The following provides a surprising but real example of how standardization in bicycle sizes can be an unexpected barrier to access a suitable bicycle. A young woman, in her early twenties, participated in the bicycle lessons. She did very well and we were keen to push her to acquire her own bicycle. For weeks her response was negative and we could not understand why, until one day she told us her dilemma. When she arrived in the Netherlands her husband, a second generation immigrant born and raised in the Netherlands, had bought her a bicycle and from day one it had been standing new and shiny in the shed, waiting to be used. It was a wedding gift and it looked beautiful. The only problem was that it was a standard size bicycle and didn't fit her. To explain to the husband why his wedding gift was not as perfect as it looked was a very delicate task.

Another element of access is service provision, in particular, parking. A substantial portion of the non-Dutch women live in neighbourhoods lacking safe parking space for bicycles near their homes. Access to equipment is about having a child-seat, panniers and other accessories generally used in the Netherlands. In order to have access you need to have information about the equipment, to know where to buy it and to determine what constitutes good quality (and therefore usability). In all these aspects lack of language skills forms a big barrier. This kind of information is typically not available in multiple languages, if it is written at all. Even if you have all the information, you also need the money to buy the equipment.

By zooming in to the three elements of motility, several social, cultural and economic factors that influence access, competence and appropriation can be identified. As participants in the courses have diverse backgrounds, the daily practice of bicycle lessons demonstrates a wide diversity of social, cultural and economic factors at play. The political context, however, is the same for the group as a whole and forms the subject of the final part of the chapter.

The Politics of Bicycle Lessons

Over the years the political framework required for the provision of bicycle lessons has turned out to be complex and tightly linked with finances (van den Langenberg, n.d.). Organizations and initiatives offering cycling courses need funding to buy bicycles that can be used during the lessons, to rent a space for meeting up, to have a budget for bicycle repair, reward volunteers involved and sometimes to hire staff to organize and/or run the lessons. As described, the potential participants tend to be women with few resources, so courses must be considered to involve minimal financial contributions from participants. Typically, personal contributions are between

€1.00 to €2.50 per lesson. In many cases local government funds part of the remaining costs, complemented by contributions from other funds or sponsors. For the organizations and people involved, this is not just about the money. To get basic funding from the local government is to get moral support. And it is exactly this moral support that a growing group of political leaders do not want to give.

Years before the financial crisis, populist politicians began to attract media attention with anti-immigrant propaganda. They stated for example that financial support from governments for separate activities for immigrant women should be stopped, and bicycle lessons and swimming lessons were used as typical examples. In an interview in *Contrast* a magazine around integration issues (Coronel, 2002), an expert in migration studies argued against the subsidized cycling lessons. He argued that cycling lessons should be open to everyone, "Outside of their own circles, in society, they will have to adapt to applicable rules". Yet at the same time in February 2002, a booklet commissioned by the Minister for Urban and Integration Policies with examples of successful integration and emancipation projects was published. One of the twenty-seven described examples was the cycling course in Tilburg: "A cycling course proves to be a simple and successful step towards a life outside of the household" (Amrit Consultancy, 2002, p. 119).

Another round of negative populist attention arose after the start of the financial crisis. Major cuts in welfare programmes were made all over the country and many initiatives for bicycle lessons had to scale down. This was not for lack of potential participants (the wish to learn to cycle continues) but simply because of a lack of financial means and support within welfare organizations, forced to narrow the focus of their provision. The Centre for Immigrant Women in Tilburg managed to keep the moral and financial support of the local government for its lessons until recently, anchored in a collaboration between the local bicycle policy and the welfare policy. Eventually, however, the Centre also had to face political reality. The populist party screened all provincial budgets, looking for projects that were specifically aimed at immigrants, and asked questions about the bicycle lessons in Tilburg. The lessons were part of the total traffic safety budget from the Province to the municipality. Even though this populist party was not part of the coalition, there was a lack of political support within the coalition on the provincial level which led to a total cut of the budget. So it is important to note that such programmes are also shaped by forces outside of their own criteria for success or failure.

Conclusion

Non-Dutch women want to overcome social, economic and cultural barriers to cycling within the context of a tumultuous political climate. With the time and support of their family, neighbours, teachers and volunteers, many of them have managed to appropriate the bicycle and make it part of their daily lives, as we see from the statistics. Close scrutiny of the factors that play a role in acquiring the necessary skills for cycling access – competences and appropriation – makes it clear that although cycling infrastructure in the Netherlands may be gender neutral, the use and image of the bicycle are not. From my own perspective as a trainer, I hope that all inhabitants in the Netherlands and elsewhere can gain access to cycling. But this requires both the building of high quality infrastructure *and* appropriate projects and courses in which people can participate in order to gain the skills and competences needed to fully utilize the bicycle.

Acknowledgements

I would like to thank all former colleagues of the Centre for Immigrant Women in Tilburg for their unconditional and ongoing support in my journey towards understanding the act and teaching of cycling, as well as all girls and women who gave me their trust and joined the lessons. The teachers and volunteers of other initiatives throughout the world, such as Cycling Schools, are another ongoing sources of inspiration and I would like to thank all of them for sharing methods, experiences, views and pictures.

References

Ajarai, H., & van Heemstra, M. (2006). *Land van Werk en Honing; Verhalen van Marokkaanse Moeders Over Hun Migratie.* Amsterdam, Netherlands: Bulaaq.

Amrit Consultancy. (2002). Fietsen als Vorm van Vrouwenemancipatie. In *Praktijkvoorbeelden van het Integratiebeleid* (pp. 119–121). Amsterdam, Netherlands: Opdracht van de Minister voor Grote Steden- en Integratiebeleid.

Arora, A. (2012). *Mobility for Equity: A Gendered Perspective on Bicycling in India.* 2012. http://designpublic.in/blog/mobility-for-equity-a-gendered-perspective-on-bicycling-in-india/ [Accessed on 20 October 2013].

Bonham, J., & Wilson, A. (2012). Women Cycling Through the Life Course: An Australian Case Study. In J. Parkin (ed.), *Cycling and Sustainability* (pp. 59–81). Bingley, UK: Emerald.

Centraal Bureau voor de Statistiek. (2012). *Statistisch Jaarboek 2012.* The Hague, Netherlands: CBS (plus online databank at http://www.cbs.nl)

Coronel, M. (2002). De Maatschappelijke Mobiliteit Komt Tot Stilstand. *Contrast, 30,* 3-10-2002.

Garrard, J., Handy, S., & Dill, J. (2012). Women and Cycling. In J. Pucher & R. Buehler (eds.), *City Cycling* (pp. 211–234). Cambridge, MA: MIT Press.

Garrard, J., Rose, G., & Sing, K.L. (2008). Promoting Transportation Cycling for Women: The Role of Bicycle Infrastructure. *Preventive Medicine, 46,* 55–59.

Grieco, M. (2006). Gender, Transport and Social Empowerment: Investigating the Consequences of the Interaction Between Gender and Constrained Mobility. In W. Ernst & U. Bohle (eds.), *Naturbilder und Lebensgrundlagen – Konstruktionen von Geschlecht, Teilband 1 Internationale Frauen- und Genderforschung in Niedersachen* (pp. 53–64). Munster, Germany: Lit Verlag Hamburg.

Hajinikitas, C. (2001). *Women and Cycling in Sydney: Determinants and Deterrents.* Results of Pilot Survey. Melbourne, Australia: Cycling Promotion Fund.

Hanson, S. (2010). Gender and Mobility: New Approaches for Informing Sustainability. *Gender, Place & Culture: A Journal of Feminist Geography, 17*(1), 5–23.

Kaufmann, V., Bergman, M.M., & Dominique, J. (2004). Motility: Mobility as Capital. *International Journal of Urban and Regional Research, 28*(4), 745–756.

Kuipers, G. (2010). *De Fiets van Hare Majesteit.* http://www.eur.nl/nieuws/detail/article/19958/ [accessed 1 September 2013].

Lehner-Lierz, U. (2003). The Role of Cycling for Women. In R. Tolley (ed.), *Sustainable Transport: Planning for Walking and Cycling in Urban Environments* (pp. 123–143). Oxford, UK: Woodhead.

Martens, K. (2013). The Role of the Bicycle in Limiting Transport Poverty in the Netherlands. In: *Proceedings of the 92nd Annual Meeting of the Transportation Research Board.* Washington, DC.

Pickup, L. (1988). Hard to Get Around: A Study of Women's Travel Mobility. In J. Little, L. Peake, & P. Richardson (eds.), *Women in Cities, Gender and the Urban Environment* (pp. 98–108). London: UK: Macmillan Education.

Polanyi, M. (1966). The Logic of Tacit Inference. *Philosophy, 41*(1), 1–18.

Pucher, J., & Buehler, R. (2008). Making Cycling Irresistible: Lessons from the Netherlands, Denmark and Germany. *Transport Reviews: A Transnational Transdisciplinary Journal, 28*(4), 495–528.

Schmidt, F.L., & Hunter, J.E. (1993). Tacit Knowledge, Practical Intelligence, General Mental Ability, and Job Knowledge, *Current Directions in Psychological Science, 2*, 8–9.

Stolovitch, H.D., & Keeps, E.J. (2002). *Telling Ain't Training.* Alexandria, VA: ASTD Press.

Van den Langenberg, S. (n.d.). *Allochtonen in het Gemeentelijk Fietsbeleid, een Analyse van Agendavorming.* Unpublished Bachelor's Thesis, Radboud Universiteit, Nijmegen, Netherlands.

Van der Kloof, A. (1996). *Stap op de Fiets! Een Verkeerscursus voor Beginnende Allochtone Fietsers.* Tilburg, Netherlands: Centrum Buitenlandse Vrouwen.

Van der Kloof, A. (2002). *Stap voor stap op de Fiets. Handleiding bij de Instructievideo voor Docenten Fietsles.* Tilburg, Netherlands: Centrum Buitenlandse Vrouwen.

Van der Kloof, A. (2003). Breaking Out by Bike: Cycling Courses as a Means of Integration and Emancipation. In Tolley, R. (ed.) *Sustainable Transport: Planning for Walking and Cycling in Urban Environments.* (pp. 650–658). Oxford, UK: Woodhead.

Van der Kloof, A. (2009). *Bicycle Training for Adults in the Netherlands. Good Practices and Methods.* Paper for Velo-city, Brussels. Available on: http://www.slideshare.net/ AvdKloof/bicycle-training-for-adults-in-the-netherlands

Van der Kloof, A. (2013). Lessons Learned Through Training Immigrant Women in the Netherlands to Cycle. Paper presented at Velo-city, Vienna 2013. Available on: http://velo-city2013.com/wp-content/uploads/20130612 _AngelaVan DerKloof.pdf

Van der Kloof, A., Bastiaanssen, J., & Martens, K. (2014). Bicycle Lessons, Activity Participation and Empowerment. In K. Lucas & A. Musso (eds.). *Social Exclusion in the Countries with Advanced Transport Systems.* Special issue of *Case Studies on Transport Policy,* 2(2), 89–95.

Wolters, S. (2011). Helpt de Fiets Allochtone Vrouwen Vooruit? Een Verkennend Onderzoek naar het Effect van Fietseducatie op de Activiteitenparticipatie van Allochtone Vrouwen. Unpublished Master's Thesis, Radboud Universiteit, Nijmegen, Netherlands.

CHAPTER 5

MAPPING EVERYDAY CYCLING IN LONDON

Brian Deegan

A map that fully represented a city's complexity and nuances would have to be to a 1:1 scale, or even larger than reality in order to reflect the multiple interpretations and uses of the spaces it depicts. As soon as the scale is zoomed inwards then assumptions, simplifications and distortions start to take place. Information is whittled down to the key determining factors and crude lines are formed. Some lines mark boundaries that cannot be crossed, whilst others form suggested routes to follow. Each map is a narrative device, conveying specifically selected sets of information, from the creator to the reader. The speed of interpretative thought required in order to distil the intended message conveyed by the mapmaker lies within the skill of the beholder. But the readability and interpretability of the map itself, is dependent on the cartographer. Base maps are created by skilled cartographers, adjusting lines at a large scale to match the oblique spheroid nature of the earth and at a small scale so that key destinations such as town centre settlements, historical monuments and public houses amongst others are referenced without overlapping text confusing the observer. How key features are determined, and which elements are considered key is part of the narrative of the map: different prioritizations tell different stories (Wood, 2010).

Does each individual in society have a preferred interpretive scale or is there a way to deliver, on a human scale, a single schematically robust representation of the larger city form for a variety of users and uses? This chapter will attempt to review London's cycling maps of the past twenty years and cycle users' interpretations of them, in order to propose a model for a new cycle mapping system. From a designer's perspective, this system should work intuitively in the hands of an individual and yet be a true reflection at a city scale of the existing conditions for cycling. To do this, an approach has been taken that draws on ethnomethodological practice, where a focus on individual experience is used as a means to uncover larger social orders. The study also draws on recent focus group research conducted as part of the wayfinding system developed for the Mayor's *Vision for Cycling*. By looking at individual cycling navigational behaviour collected from these focus groups, as well as personal informal encounters and participant observation, a system is suggested that contains the information cyclists actually need and in a form they can easily understand.

The cycle route map in London at present is a politically sensitive topic (Sherwin & Melia, 2012) and, as frequently occurs in such cases, design influences beyond plain service functioning are present in the production of the maps. It should be no surprise to recognize that mapping is a contested practice: its history is loaded with contestation and meaning. Maps never simply convey uncontested data, but the stories they tell are active participants in the places they depict. City maps designed for cyclists undergo frequent revision, not just to reflect changes in the environments they seek to depict, but in the elements included and excluded. More information can result in less readability. Too much simplification can render a map meaningless in use. Cities such as Copenhagen and Brussels have long utilized user feedback to assist in the decision making around city map reproduction and even a brief comparison of different iterations demonstrates how much this is contested.

So what makes a cycling map a cycling map rather than any other kind of map? Perhaps at its simplest, a map is a graphical way of presenting information on any given topic(s) for a particular audience. The aim may be to cram as much information into the visual dimension as possible, or to simplify it to the absolute minimum. Similarly, the intended readership may be specialist or general. Each map does not simply mirror a pre-existing reality but helps shape how we perceive that which we encounter. How are different elements prioritized, and which elements are deemed suitable to be mentioned? The CTC Route Books of the 1890s were provided with minimalist maps that simply sketched the roads themselves. Relevant information – on surfaces, warnings about steep hills, things to look for to help navigation, potential refreshment stops – were all contained in the text of the books themselves. These were route guides to assist a leisured new class of riders to get the most out of their days out, a format which persists in the provision of route guides today (for a range of means of touring). But to provide maps as part of a strategy to encourage greater levels of urban transport, cycling poses a very different set of problems to those met by the route guides. By their very nature, journeys for commuting and other basic quotidian transport functions are fragmented and individualized. Flows and aggregate data can be measured to assess relative levels of demand, but how can maps facilitate these journeys, and form a meaningful part of a strategy for increasing urban transport cycling? And in doing so, how might they reflect the different needs of the variety of people who cycle in any given city and the range of journey types they are making?

The term *cyclist* carries a lot of cultural baggage in the UK. As a label it not only functions as a means of solidarity (see discussion in Chapter 1, this volume) but also as an homogenizing descriptor, imposed from outside. Like any label it can function not simply as a neutral identifier of a certain group of persons, but as a means to draw a relatively impermeable barrier around that group to identify those who belong and do not belong. In Transport for London's latest *Attitudes to Cycling* report only 44% of non-cyclists considered cyclists to be considerate, 38% considered cyclists to be law abiding, 37% considered cyclists to be like themselves and 43% considered them to be dangerous (TfL, 2013a). Put simply, the prevailing attitude among those who identify themselves as "non-cyclists" seems to be that "cyclists" are inconsiderate, law- breaking, abnormal, maniacs. According to the logic exhibited here the diverse range of people and activity are homogenized in popular discourse into a single social group that poses a problem for majority society. Adopting a voice of authority: "How then are these *rebels* to be managed and organized and perhaps kept out of the way of normal people going about their hard working, considerate lives?" This is a conspiratorial summary of authority but politicians are, in large part, aware of the prevailing social norms and will try to reflect them. Hence, top-down analyses of cycling cultures can become so laden with myth and stereotype as to be unfathomable. That being said, much research has been done on the positive impact of cycling. However, even some positive research can be laden with preconceived prejudices, as much research, especially in the UK, is orientated towards addressing established negative social norms about this species of humans called "cyclists".

Here, perhaps we see the greatest contrast with the situations discussed in previous chapters examining policy and politics in the Netherlands. While negative attitudes towards those who ride may be visible in popular and some political discourse there, there is a broader consensus to ensure that this does not become the dominant discourse. While practical matters such as cycle parking and congestion can prove problematic, city governments and citizens alike are aware that their cities could not function if people were discouraged from travelling by bicycle. Cycle travel is a means to ensure the social sustainability of travel as much as it is a means to ensure increased environmental sustainability. While visionary strate-gists exist within the UK, they operate in broader political frameworks where these primary assumptions are absent (Pooley et al 2013, p. 169). The unique governance structure of

London within the UK, and its desire to remain internationally competitive as a site for business investment, means that its transport policy has been much more strongly influenced by Europe-wide trends in urban mobility policies and practices. Coupled with a consistent and vigorous set of grass-roots campaigns for cycling since the 1970s (see Cox, 2015), we can see why cycling in London has a unique status in the UK, and why the provision of cycle-specific maps has been an integral part of strategies to either contain or encourage bicycle use in the capital. Maps and mapping are as subject to the expression of prejudice as any other process in society. Decision makers will inevitably want their personal ideas about informing cyclists' behaviour represented in the printed form, especially on something they hope cyclists will view every day. In 2005, for example, the City of London issued a map for cyclists. It was ostensibly designed to encourage cycle use, but at the same time as showing route information, it contained a list of constraints and instructions that clearly indicated preconceptions made about its prospective readers and further, sought to discipline them as a particular type of citizen, by demanding they wear helmets and high-visibility clothing, not jump red traffic signals and so on. The advice clearly already had an image of riders as a certain class of dangerous, undisciplined persons. It is these sets of preconceptions prevalent in recent historical approaches to cycling policy that need to be set aside, in order to gain a better insight into what people actually do. In relation to maps providing routing information for the urban traveller, it is invaluable to examine actual individual navigational behaviour before forming conclusions about the social order and how mapping systems may, or may not, assist cyclists in as clear a way as possible. The aim should be to assist cyclists' wayfinding methods, not sit in judgement on their behaviour.

Cycle Maps of London

Before we embark on our examination it seems like a sensible idea to review London's cycle maps produced in the current policy context and their place within a transport strategy for the city. The Greater London Authority was established in 2000, with Transport for London (TfL) formed as a body able to co-ordinate policy across the city region. For the sixteen years prior to that, London Regional Transport (responsible for public transport) was answerable directly to the Secretary of State for Transport, a cabinet post held by nine different incumbents during that time. Cycling policy (such as there was) fell under general road transport policy so there was little meaningful policy co-ordination. With the foundation of TfL, however, came the possibility to put a cycling strategy in place as part of a broader transport strategy. This is a chequered history, but if a city or town wishes to be considered *cycling friendly* then at the most basic level two things are required in the context of transport policy and strategy; one, that they have some infrastructural provision for cycling (of whatever form is appropriate) and two, that this provision is mapped and made public along with an indication of the prevailing attitudes towards cycling and the current strategy for cycling (Dekoster & Schollaert, 1999).

The following section considers the content of cycle maps in London and the efforts by those who produced them both to reflect and affect social norms. The majority of London's transport policy leaders have been making a concerted effort for a number of years for the City to be considered a *cycle friendly* city or, to use the phrase adopted by the Mayor of London in 2008 from the London Cycling Campaign, a "Cyclised" city. Cycling has therefore officially been presented as a means to civilize an area, as opposed to it being seen as an antisocial nuisance.

Responsibility for cycling policy delivery is currently delegated to local authorities in London, of which there are thirty-three (thirty-two borough councils plus the City of London Corporation). These produce individual cycle maps alongside TfL's own London-wide coverage. Local maps provide a schematic summary of each borough's current, and in some cases, proposed, infrastructure. Information and images presented on the reverse of each map provide interesting insights into how the local authority actually views cycling. Earlier cycling maps, however, had also been produced by grass-roots campaigning organizations. Most notable of these is the London Cycling Campaign formed in 1978 to bring together a number of local campaigning groups formed earlier in the decade.

Rather than seek to list, present and analyse each sample map individually, the following pages identify a typology of approaches to map presentation. In order to make these groupings and to construct the typology, two ways of thinking are brought together. First, the discussions of social norms, derived from the work of Alan Berkowicz, with the refinements suggested by Cialdini et al. (2000). Simply summarized, they consider norms to be those patterns of behaviour accepted as normal (that is, unremarkable) within any given society. To put cycling in the UK into context within this schema we can recall the research conducted by the Transport Research Laboratory (TRL) in 2002 examining drivers' attitudes towards cycling. The classification summary ended up employing categories such as "despised", "arrogant", "irresponsible" and "dangerous". At that point in time, drivers could only think of two positive things to say about cyclists: that they were "healthy" and "brave" (Basford et al., 2002).

Cialdini et al. (2000) distinguish between different types of norm. For our purposes, since the perspectives under scrutiny here are primarily those of local authorities, the injunctive norm is of most relevance. Injunctive norms express what most people are perceived to approve of. The publication of cycle maps gives authorities opportunities to demonstrate what they consider as broader social norms in the way they frame cycling activities supported by such maps. Social norm theory suggests that this affects people's behaviour, even if what is presented is not actually the case. Put simply, if the individual believes that everyone believes it, then that is usually enough.

In order to make a typology of map archetypes, building on the way that normative assumptions are made and displayed, we can make further use of Everett Rogers' work on the diffusion of innovations (2003). Rogers attempts to explain how new ideas are filtered through society over time. Although cycling could hardly be classed as a new innovation, its rein-vention in recent years as a tool for social improvement in terms of health, economy, climate change, democratization and quality of life (Cycling England, 2007) certainly requires some innovative thought and rebranding. Furthermore, as has pre-viously been pointed out, the negligible rates of transport cycling in the UK mean that any initial map to propose cycle commuting is propounding an innovative activity. Rogers suggests that there are five process stages towards accepting a new innovation; knowledge, persuasion, decision, implementa-tion and confirmation. The argument is that these five stages can also be used to provide a typology of London cycling maps as they discursively reflect and project changing norms and public perceptions.

These five stages can be understood as ideal types exhibited in the different maps produced. This is not to say that the standard of cycle maps is generally improving, just that the information presented and the way it is presented, is changing. Importantly, these changes demonstrate growing acceptance of cycling as a viable and mainstream mode of transport. Technically speaking, there is very little difference between the first map reviewed and the last, in terms of the methodology used, but their messages reflect a shift towards cycling being accepted as a social norm.

A Typology of Cycle Maps

> We know we will win the battle eventually but sometimes victory seems a long way off.

> (London Cycling Campaign Cycle Map, 1992)

Knowledge maps

The first stage of diffusion is to ensure the spread of basic knowledge. Initial presentations of cycle-specific maps engage with their readership almost as a mission statement or manifesto: to engage interest and to provide a guerrilla guide to cycling in a hostile and largely uninviting environment. They are created to suggest possibilities in a situation where specific needs of cyclists are barely considered. The London Cycling Campaign map produced in 1992 is a good example. Notably, it contains information about where your cycle is likely to be removed if you park it illegally. Useful information certainly, and suggestions made in this 1992 map are almost exactly the same as they are today. Key cycling corridors, or, more accurately, less hostile corridors remain the same today as they were twenty-three years ago.

Persuasive maps

The second stage of diffusion is designed to entice prospective adopters by demonstrating the potential future prospects and benefits. In terms of cycle maps these show glimpses of a utopian future, albeit one potentially many years into the future. Those produced for the London Cycling Network from the late 1990s until 2002 are good examples. They show both completed and planned sections of network. Cyclists reading these are given messages to enable them to envisage a future when the route at the end of their road does not simply evaporate with the ubiquitous "cyclists dismount" (or, alternatively "end of route") sign, but actually runs into an interconnected network of high quality cycle routes making journeys across the capital as simple as driving in a car. In reality, the routes never did all join up and getting in a car remains the most rational choice for many Londoners, particularly those in outer London boroughs.

Decision maps

The third type is best represented by the Transport for London Cycle Guides, produced from 2004 to the present. These maps show route differentiation and classification. The reader is introduced to advisory information on quiet, less trafficked routes. It is implicit that these are preferable for riding. The inference is that users are rational agents making informed route decisions and so require decision-making information. A once utopian, one size fits all model, is replaced with a practical guide to an embedded reality. Realistic accuracy is preferable to a simple line for some, but some "quiet" routes show travel on major traffic arteries and so questions of misleading information arise (Sherwin et al., 2012).

Implementation maps

As an innovation spreads, people know about it, and want to use it, so the logical next process step is in the form of specific forms of implementation. This type is best exemplified by the Cycle Hire maps which, until recently, showed simply a series of points where mass transit utility in the form of hireable cycles could be obtained. One piece of simple information is shown in order to reflect the efficiency and simplicity of the system. The cycle hire maps were planned and delivered based on a 500 m by 500 m grid system. Central London itself is the route network, with each individual free to decide their own route and destiny, as long as bikes are dropped at certain randomly available points. The map presents cycling as a blank utilitarian transport choice, removed from prejudice and cultural stereotypes. Put simply, the hired service you requested and paid for can be picked up here and dropped off there. Everything else is presented as a value-free matter of choice.

Confirmation maps

The final type has yet to be produced in London so far, but the rest of this chapter aims to unlock what such a map could be like. What would a map that properly reflects actual and desired riding look like? To do this, we first have to go back to the makers of the first map; the people who *do* cycle in London. We should then find out how they plot their journeys in practice and only then should we consider the analytical methods to employ. Greg Rybarczyk's 2014 study "Simulating bicycle wayfinding mechanisms in an urban environment" examined how urban cyclists navigate: what aspects of the built environment do people actually use? The research tested several changes to the urban form and concluded that there are positive correlations between certain aspects of street design and the ability of cyclists to navigate successfully. This is a great example of model-testing and helps inform professionals on how best to design and plan streets for cyclists. However, being design-led, its limitation is that improvement demands change. Action is required by authorities in order for a successful wayfinding system to be enabled. This section first attempts to uncover the tips, tricks and skills that existing cyclists already use, based on their specific local circumstances, in order to plot their way around town. Second, it considers whether these can be replicated in the format of a schematic map in order to help new cyclists plot their own way through the maze. Such a map would function as a confirmation-type map.

In 2010, Transport for London undertook some cycling wayfinding research and suggested some wayfinding principles developed from cyclist interviews. Most of these were generic items covering, safety, coherence, security, positivity, control and inclusivity but one of the principles related to the use of the knowledge of individual cyclists. It is from these latter unpublished findings together with additional study data, that the following analysis is derived. From 2014 TfL conducted a survey of 703 cyclists and when respondents were asked about wayfinding, only 8% said they used cycling-specific maps during their journey (TfL, 2010). Since 2010, many cyclists have acquired mobile phones with GPS tracking applications and so today this number is likely to be even lower.

In relation to the knowledge principle, the Transport for London research concluded that any wayfinding system developed for cyclists should not distort their existing knowledge but instead should add to it. This suggestion poses a conundrum for cycle network planners. A superimposed form that looks elegant at a macro planning level, such as a grid or a series of concentric circles, may not be useful at street level where the macro view is not possible. The Cycle Superhighways in London, designed as mid-range radial routes are a good example. They are based on an image of a clock face, with central London as the centre of the clock. Hence, twelve routes were conceived each representing a clock face number. At a macro level, this is an elegant approach that makes sense to funders and decision makers. Yet at street level, a superhighway may be confusing when encountered by a cyclist. Its lack of connections would make little sense and its placement may seem random and unjustified in relation to potential usage.

So How Do People Get Around?

Bike trips to work in London represent 3.9% of the total work commutes in the capital and approximately 600,000 cycling trips are made every day (ONS, 2014). This is approximately the same number of cyclists as Amsterdam and so is not a statistically insignificant outlying proportion of population. What do these cyclists use in order to navigate? Do they use maps, do they use apps or do they just figure it out? The author of this chapter is employed to conceive, plan and deliver cycle networks. But he is also a bicycle rider in London who has had to develop his own patterns of wayfinding. Reflexive analysis of the knowledge required to do this on a personal level led to a series of personal interviews and focus groups on the subject and the formation of the methods shown below. Cyclists in London have developed some of these methods in an almost subconscious manner. Just as with Angela van der Kloof's observations on the knowledge required to ride (Chapter 3 in this volume) the unconscious competences involved in getting around have to be uncovered. Understanding these processes may allow us to consider differently how to present cycle mapping.

Ethnomethodologists make sense of the world through the analysing of individual day-to-day experiences (Garfinkel, 1967). These experiences are then examined in order to gain an understanding of wider social order. It is a method that starts without a model or any preconceived ideas, just gathers data in order to see what patterns emerge. For this reason it was selected as an appropriate and useful way to examine the variety of practices and expectations of cycling exhibited by those who ride in London. In order to observe the methods used by cyclists, focus group research was undertaken in August 2014 in which groups of six existing cyclists were asked to interpret the information on a cycle map. The map used was a TfL cycle guide: an A0 map with routes highlighted in different colours on an A–Z style basemap. The majority of participants, when presented with this large map, found the information confusing, cumbersome and daunting. The general feeling was that there was too much information. If lost, they all preferred using their phones to see where they were and where they needed to get to. The printed cycle map is a long-standing institution but perhaps in the face of new mapping technologies it is more for cycle network planning enthusiasts than actual cyclists.

In light of the above reflections, it was decided that rather than asking cyclists to engage with a preconceived model, it might be better to ask experienced cyclists how they navigate.

Mapping Everyday Cycling in London

Years of anecdotes and advice gained from correspondence and conversation with hundreds of cyclists on this subject has led the author to make the following observations about the variety of practices evident among the varied social groups that ride. Each section here reflects a different set of wayfinding practices, and is introduced with a reference reflecting the tone of the comment as it was first received. The examples discussed are specific to the respondents' experiences of riding in London, but the principles exposed may be transferable to other cities, not just in the UK.

Along where the old Thames does flow

Central London cyclists tend to navigate around central London by using the River Thames as a reference point. The River Thames is one of London's most famous landmarks and neatly divides South London from North London. The river runs mainly east–west through the city but due to its lower course geological status it meanders into north–south alignments as well. Despite this limitation as a route guide, it remains a key geographical reference point for cyclists. In many cyclists' own mental maps, if they can keep a feeling of where the river is, then central London navigation is more straightforward.

East–west bridge orientation

Some cyclists take this a step further and use their knowledge of the bridges and the best route alignments with them in order to create a virtual grid. If you know where the river is and you know which bridge crossing you are in line with, then you have a clear understanding of where you are, based on a few pieces of information. Many of the routes leading to bridges used by cyclists are not necessarily the main road corridors but back streets where difficult situations involving mixing with heavy or fast streams of motor traffic can be avoided. The route to the north of Waterloo Bridge along Wellington Street through Covent Garden is a great example, as is Queen's Street to the north of Southwark Bridge. When bridges are aligned with access to quieter roads then these tend to become heavily populated with cyclists.

The shadow of Roman Britain

Another observation made is that cyclists orientate to Roman roads. If you examine the street pattern of London then urban morphological forms based on historical approaches to settlement design present themselves. Medieval street design is considered haphazard in the modern world struggling to give motor vehicle transport space to move and park, but so many streets in London run in a north–west to south-east alignment that a simpler form presents itself. Hyde Park to St Albans is the classic Roman design line and surrounding roads all seem to match this pattern as they were built as parallel connectors. Likewise, the City of London to Chelmsford is another Roman desire-line for those heading east-west. Many roads conform to this alignment, several of them directly. Cyclists who find themselves on a main road in North London and know this morphology would instantly know their orientation. Cyclists, powered by the expenditure of personal energy, desire as-the-crow-flies journeys more than any other transport mode. The London Cycle Network Plus programme attempted to address this by establishing priority strategic routes in straight lines between town centre settlements. As many of these corridors were already claimed for main road traffic, however, compromises in quality were inevitable (Deegan & Parkin, 2011).

All roads lead to Hyde Park

A further examination of London's street orientation reveals that many roads gravitate towards Hyde Park, which acts as a nodal point upon which cycle routes converge. Hyde Park is the motorway of London cycling with flows of a magnitude comparable to any city on earth. This is in large part due to this orientation. Anyone heading towards central London from any compass point will find himself or herself honing in on Hyde Park. It seemed essential to every cyclist interviewed to have a strategy for passing through it.

On reaching Hyde Park, general traffic is circulated around the park often using several carriageway lanes. Cyclists are permitted to use certain routes within the park: these become high cycle flow situations. Parks are not designed to handle large volumes of vehicular traffic, even bicycle. Consequently, problems arise, especially conflict with pedestrians. The inevitability of using Hyde Park on a cycle trip has led to some cyclists plotting different entrances and exits such as Stanhope Gate on the northern side, which has a signalized, and parallel to pedestrians, crossing facility. This crossing provides entry to and exit from Hyde Park across the busy Bayswater Road. Local cyclists campaigned for years to put this crossing in place so that they could avoid the general traffic flows at Hyde Park Corner and Marble Arch. This route remains the park's best kept secret and is the pleasant route option for experienced cyclists wishing to avoid motor vehicle and mass cycling conflicts.

Follow the flow
Cycling is a peak-time commuter activity in London. Cyclists comprise 24% of central London peak-time traffic (Office for National Statistics, ONS, 2014). Human beings are inherently social animals according to Aristotle and few would argue against this. It is therefore unsurprising that cyclists will tend to follow other cyclists heading in similar direction. This can lead to the rider discovering more efficient routes or potential new cut-through routes to their destination. During peak-time, a sensible strategy could be to follow the flow and use this to plot your journey along an established cycling corridor. Many back streets in central London have an 80%+ mode share for cyclists (TfL, 2013b). It is important to note when thinking about cycle networks – as opposed to general highway networks – that an

121

unassuming street of low significance in terms of road hierarchy classification can be functioning as a trunk road for cycle traffic. Colebrooke Row in Islington is a good example of this as cyclists heading south from the north or north-east all seem to converge on one back street in the morning peak as it aligns itself with a quiet yet direct road into the City of London. This route avoids a gyratory system and a large multi-lane roundabout at Angel and Old Street respectively. Many of the strategic corridors for cycling in London have been formed this way: this type of knowledge eventually filters through to local authority officers who may choose to adopt these routes into the cycle network.

Avoid main roads like the plague
Some cyclists plot ways to get around town without ever having to cycle on main roads. This requires some strong strategic thought about how best to tackle areas or avoid them altogether. The Wembley area, in particular, is difficult to approach from the south without some element of main road cycling. It seems almost like a badge of honour for cyclists who plot their way around using this method. An intricate knowledge of the cycle networks and an ability to test and fail repeatedly appear to be prerequisites for this method of wayfinding.

A crossing worth bearing in mind
Good crossing points of major roads can be a godsend to cyclists. This approach was common to all experienced cyclists interviewed. They all knew where "best" to cross and the most effective strategy for getting from area to area unscathed. These points are referenced as Gateways in the latest London Cycling Design Standards (TfL, 2014) and, like the Colebrooke Row example mentioned earlier, they provide comfortable, easily rideable ways of bypassing potentially problematic links. In the case of Colebrooke Row, the problem is the six lanes of traffic comprising City Road. When cyclists approach City Road from Colebrooke Row they can cross exclusively within their own

stage in the signal operation. Other examples include the Ossulton Street crossing of Euston Road where, again, six lanes of traffic are crossed heading south whilst avoiding the compulsory left turn for general traffic. Stanhope Gate, also mentioned earlier, is another example and there are dozens more scattered across London. Remembering these nodal points is a lot easier than remembering the orientation of routes through maze-like backstreets, so many experienced cyclists seem to navigate by making sure they hit certain points. This is one of the key pieces of knowledge that an experienced cyclist can pass on to a new cyclist. It will have the biggest impact on the quality of their journey. If cyclists had another 200 of these points then all of London could be easily accessible by bike. Importantly, this is a navigational principle clearly transferable to other cities, where cyclists ride without comprehensive segregated infrastructure.

Cognitive transport clues
Some cyclists reference other navigation systems (such as bus stops, street names, main destination signing and Legible London signs) whilst in transit. Bus stops have a referenced destination and, most of the time, it will be in the direction of travel. This technique can come unstuck on one-way systems but seems to be a good clue to pick up on when riding. Street naming conventions can work on an area basis and locally, if you have enough knowledge. Like rivers, streets lead to roads and roads lead to high roads or high streets so an area location can be ascertained. Highway signs intended for cars are also useful but these will tend to avoid known cycle routes, which often run in parallel to main road corridors. Or they may, for traffic management purposes, take cyclists on wide detours since many local authorities attempt to avoid congestion by filtering mass motor traffic though certain streets. Highway signs are, however, particularly useful as navigation aids. Legible London map totems are a very useful new addition to

the city's signage as the map face is orientated with the direction you are looking. In order to analyse these properly cyclists have to stop and (usually) mount the kerb but a quick glance from the carriageway can reveal the orientation of green spaces, rivers, bridges, railway lines or other barriers or landmarks that could help with orientation and navigation.

Main road certainty

Urban transport cyclists prefer a consistent level of service, where they can rely on a route. Main roads are seldom closed, allow cyclists to go fast without constant stopping and are usually on the most direct alignment. Main roads are usually well lit and tend to be overlooked by commercial activity during the day and by residents at night, so they are the most socially safe of roads. The presence of car drivers can be a comfort to cyclists since, at night in particular, some back street cycle routes can be intimidating due to their isolation. The initial cycle superhighways tried to utilize main road alignments in order to satisfy the fast commuter cyclists who do not necessarily want to make too many decisions but instead prefer to flow with general traffic. It is very hard to get lost when sticking to main roads and so this is an effective navigational strategy. It is, however, perhaps the hardest method to use in order to entice new people to take up cycling.

Inquisitive exploration.

Some interviewed cyclists professed to encountering on-street signs, usually London Cycle Network signs, and following them, more out of curiosity than expectancy. When doing so, they often uncovered pleasant alternative routes to the main road alignments with which they may have previously been more familiar. For example, when one interviewee discovered a route along Arlington Street in Camden, which runs parallel to the much busier Hampstead Road, they were delighted. Despite running right next to the busy mainline Euston Station this street carried little traffic and provided a straight across signalized movement to traverse the busy Euston Road. Their previous route (Hampstead Road) when heading south leads to Tottenham Court Road – four lanes of one-way oncoming traffic – and the Euston underpass – a two lane slip road down to another emerging two lanes. Following the blue London Cycle Network signs was like following a Hansel and Gretel style dropped breadcrumb trail but one which proved a saviour. Despite the prevalence of London Cycle Network Signs out on London streets, few actual cyclists reference them and when they do, it can seem more out of curiosity. Cycle route signage can therefore lead to discoveries of potentially great routes. Unfortunately, due to past in-consistent infrastructure delivery standards, they can just as likely lead cyclists to dismount points or narrow shared footways and so all but a few of the routes are held in deep suspicion by most cyclists interviewed.

Most of these techniques become obsolete if the cyclist has a working smartphone and does not mind losing momentum enough to refer to a mapping system showing their current location. However, if phone network coverage is poor or the phone has fallen victim to its short battery life then these navigational tips still prove useful. The argument made here is that for a mapping system to make sense, it should be based on the knowledge of those already successfully navigating the streets, not the abstract clarity of an imposed planning strategy. Established cycle networks can take up to thirty years to fully bed-in. As London is at the start of its journey to take cycling seriously as a mainstream mode of transport then a system reflecting the best known local information could prove useful. London is also in the habit of changing its approach to cycle network delivery every five years and so cyclists could consider that learning a system would be a waste of effort.

Conclusions

What then would a cycle map look and feel like if it were based on methods derived from this examination of personal cycle navigational methods? Perhaps a grid system using east–west routes starting with the Thames as its route zero and north–south routes aligned along pleasant routes leading to each of London's bridges might help. Perhaps a focus on opening up crossing points and highlighting these to existing and potential cyclists through the adaptation of existing wayfinding systems such as Legible London or even through a *find my nearest gateway* app. Perhaps cycle routes should be plotted that follow the alignments of roads as they were delivered historically so that they minimize the number of turns and *doglegs* associated with cutting across the form of the street. The questions posed by this analysis suggest further research is needed if commuters are to be aided and encouraged on to and through the streets of London by bike.

Perhaps also a new science could be born uniting personal cycling user knowledge with the study of urban morphology in order to deliver mapping and city planning practices to facilitate the growth of cycling. Starting principles could relate mapping information to established categories of urban form. For example, if street density is coarse, then routes could be utilized where as in finer street forms points could be utilized. Areas with high buildings would need street based navigational aids, usually in the form of on-street signs, whereas open spaces could lead to more map-based navigation focused on key identifiable features. Areas with high population densities may require disaggregated parallel networks away from roads reserved mainly for service vehicles with clear and frequent on-street signs. Whereas in low population areas highway signs may be a simpler navigational aid. Areas with a mono function could be best served by a wayfinding system that blended in with existing signing approaches: in mixed function areas a greater degree of conspicuity may be needed for each use.

When London has a 400 by 400 m grid-scaled, identifiable high quality well signed cycle network (as is the basis of provision in the Netherlands) then navigation may simplify itself to just heading in any direction until you hit a network route. However, at present there are only a few easily identifiable comfortable corridors for cycling in London, so individual mental maps will have to be used for a long time to come. A single elegant, logically planned route-based system requires commitment to building a full network infrastructure to back it up. In European cities with longer established mass cycling cultures, wayfinding makes sense: cyclists are guaranteed a certain level of service on the routes suggested. In the author's opinion, London planners have a history of wanting to head towards the system without putting in the groundwork. The findings here suggest that as a first step, more crossings of difficult roads should be implemented and an initial route network adapted to these nodes. Only when a clear picture of how this will look becomes evident, can schematic representations be derived. Until then, key safe crossing points recommended by cyclists should be highlighted to other cyclists in any developed mapping system. It would be a relatively simple procedure to highlight these crossing points on a phone app and link them to a suggested journey.

London is a long way off abandoning a knowledge-based system of how best to avoid the excesses of motorized traffic and moving to an intuitive and understandable network. Put simply, you have to build a good product before you do the marketing. We need to look at the form, function and quality of the streets and fully commit to moulding a network around them. Mapping, and the routing processes associated with it, is far from an objective process. Maps make assumptions and both reflect and shape social norms. Perhaps it is worth considering the instructional text on the reverse face of the 2014 City of Copenhagen cycle map (with its linked smartphone routeplanner app) whose first of six "biking dogmas" is "Spread Positive Karma".

References

Basford, L., Reid, S., Lester, T., Thomson, J., & Tolmie, A. (2002). Driver's Perceptions of Cyclists [TRL549] Transport Research Laboratory, UK (http://www.trl.co.uk).

Cialdini, R., Kallgren, C., & Reno, R. (2000). A Focus Theory of Normative Conduct: When Norms Do and Do Not Affect Behavior. *Personality and Social Psychology Bulletin,* October 2000, 26: 1002–1012.

Cox, P. (2015). Cycling, Environmentalism and Change in 1970s Britain. Paper presented at Mobility and Environment Conference, 13–14 February 2015, Kerschensteiner Kolleg, Deutsches Museum, Munich.

Cycling England. (2007). *Valuing the benefits of cycling* http://webarchive.nationalarchives.gov.uk/201104070946 07/http:/www.dft.gov.uk/cyclingengland/site/wp-content/uploads/2008/08/valuing-the-benefits-of-cycling-full.pdf

Deegan, B. & Parkin, J. (2011). Planning Cycling Networks: Human Factors and Design Processes. *Proceedings of the ICE – Engineering Sustainability, 164*(1), 85–93.

Dekoster, J., & Schollaert, U. (1999). *Cycling: The Way Ahead for Towns and Cities.* Brussels: European Commission. http://ec.europa.eu/environment/archives/cycling/cycling_en.pdf

Garfinkel, H. (1967). *Studies in Ethnomethodology.* Englewood Cliffs, NJ: Prentice-Hall.

Office for National Statistics (ONS), (2014) *2011 Census Analysis – Cycling to Work* (released 26 March 2014) http://www.ons.gov.uk/ons/dcp171776_357613.pdf

Pooley, C., Jones, T., Tight, M., Horton, D., Scheldeman, G., Jopson, A., & Strano, E. (2013). *Promoting Walking and Cycling: New Perspectives on Sustainable Travel*. Bristol: Policy Press.

Rogers, E.M. (2003). *Diffusion of Innovations* (fifth edition). New York: Free Press.

Rybarczyk, G. (2014). Simulating Bicycle Wayfinding Mechanisms in an Urban Environment. *Urban Planning and Transport Research*, 2(1) 89–104.

Sherwin, H., & Melia, S. (2012). *Cycle Mapping in the UK and the 'London Cycle Map'*. Project Report. Ideas in Transit, http://ideasintransit.org.

Transfers. (2013). Special Section on Rickshaws. 3(3).

Transport for London (TfL). 2010. Wayfinding Study (unpublished).

Transport for London (TfL). (2013a). *Attitudes to Cycling*. From: http://www.clocs.org.uk/wp-content/uploads/2014/05/Attitudes-to-Cycling-March-2013-Report-FINAL-FOR-LIBRARY.pdf.

Transport for London (TfLb). (2013). Central London Cycle Census, from http://www.tfl.gov.uk/cdn/static/cms/documents /cycle-census-technical-note.pdf

Transport for London (TfL), (2014). Cycle Wayfinding Research (unpublished).

Wood, D. (2010). *Rethinking the Power of Maps*. New York: The Guilford Press.

CHAPTER 6

CARGO BIKES:
DISTRIBUTING CONSUMER GOODS

Peter Cox and Randy Rzewnicki

Introduction

Any commodity destined for individual purchase and use will undergo a long distribution chain from producer to consumer. Given the combination of mass production and a mass-consumption society, distribution patterns can be seen as dendritic, spreading from manufacturer to buyer, involving ever finer levels of dispersal and reduction in numbers, alongside ever more diverse modes of distribution. There are, of course, other commodity flows between sources and raw materials and production, and of labour within these processes. This chapter considers the role of human powered vehicles: bicycles and tricycles, in this mundane distribution of consumer goods. Bulk-produced, quotidian items, from foodstuffs to newspapers to clothing are consumed at an individual and household level and cargo bikes of a variety of designs have long been envisaged as part of this chain of commodity distribution from retailer to consumer.

The problem of luggage carrying was recognized from the very earliest days of the bicycle, and various forms of pannier, basket, rack and bag arrangements can be seen, dating back as far as 1817 when a luggage platform was an integral feature of many draisines – the "running machines" usually considered as the precursors of the pedal driven bicycle (Hadland & Lessing, p. 353). In a satirical set of drawings commenting on the new craze for velocipedes, the Leipzig *Illustrierte Zeitung* of 3 July 1869, carried a sketch of a wheelbarrow-velocipede hybrid, complete with cargo of an unfeasibly large sausage. Actual cycles designed expressly for commercial goods carriage have been around since the 1880s. Classic examples include the production of cycles for newspaper distribution, for post office use, and for retailers of foodstuffs: butchers, bakers and grocers, as well those used by individual vendors selling to passing pedestrians. From the late 1970s, within a more individualized consumer culture, the transporter cycle has re-emerged as a personal vehicle in Denmark, the Netherlands and elsewhere: property of the consumer household rather than the retailer. Finally, in the twenty-first century, we are seeing the cargo bike returning as a commercial delivery vehicle as retailing patterns change again in a digital communications era, and logistics becomes a major concern. This chapter maps the changing fortunes of cargo bikes not simply as design objects, but in relation to, and as a function of, changing forms of retail and consumer culture. It demonstrates that to understand the fortunes of some forms of cycling we must look beyond the fascination of the technology itself and understand its place within wider cultural changes here, in particular, by studying the changing face of consumer culture and its role in society.

Interest in sustainable mobility has drawn attention to the "last mile" journey of consumer goods (Edwards et al., 2009). The "last mile" refers both to final delivery to the customer at the end of the entire production, distribution and retail chain, and the redistribution of goods from the point of purchase to the point of use by the customer/consumer. In reality, of course, it is very rarely a last mile and can be a considerable distance indeed. With neo-liberalism producing cities that are "increasingly defined by elites through and by consumption", this final redistribution of goods is increasingly crucial as a means by which the character of the urban environment is, and can be, defined and redefined (Miles, 2012, p. 216). Yet it is also clear that the mobility patterns of the final dispersal of goods are intimately bound up with the character of shops and the processes of shopping as they have changed over the past 150 years.

The emergence of a sociology of consumption (see e.g. the *Journal of Consumer Culture*) has refocused attention on the history of shops and shopping, but has tended to emphasize issues of place and identity in the consumer (e.g. Miller et al., 1998). Historical studies provide valuable data on changing patterns of retail but again, emphasis in these is more on retail and consumption rather than distribution (see e.g. Strasser et al., 1998; Bowlby, 2001; Graham, 2008; Francks & Hunter, 2012). To map the changing fortunes of cargo bikes in their various forms, this chapter utilizes a range of sources. First, it employs manufacturers' descriptions of their machines, and draws from contemporary reports of their uses in trade, press and other cyclists' magazines. Second, it builds on existing academic studies of the history of shops and shopping. A third element, used with some caution, is the range of accounts compiled by enthusiasts. These literary sources are combined with insights from within a current international project on the use of cargo bikes in sustainable urban transport, allowing insights into the policy arena and discussions from an insider perspective. Although the specific details and the material on the earlier history of retail are largely drawn from the UK, the international nature of the bicycle trade allows us to make a number of comparative observations (Burr, 2012). The more recent resurgence of cargo bikes has become transnational in scope although retaining distinctive local characteristics and so the final sections of the chapter also draw on practitioner accounts of the promotion and current use of cargo bikes.

As a relatively invisible transport mode, much of the historical evidence is often fragmentary and passing, drawn from the marginalia of secondary sources and photographic records. Studying these machines and their use is further complicated by the complete lack of common nomenclature.

Throughout the chapter, the general terms *cargo bike* or *carrier cycle* are employed, with note of, and use made of, local and historic terminology where appropriate, and specific terms as applied to particular vehicle types where necessary. As Hadland and Lessing (2014, p. 380) put it, "Cargo bikes are also known as freightbikes, carrier cycles, work bikes, and tradesman's bikes and are sometimes referred to generically as delibikes, baker's bikes, or butcher's bikes": and this only in the English language. Among this profusion, we should be reminded that many of the designs do not have two wheels and for many others, the cargo may be human passengers rather than inert goods.

Origins

In one of the few academic studies of working cycles, Norcliffe (2011) sketches their origins to James Starley's three tricycle designs of 1877, all of which could be adapted to carry either passengers or goods. In parallel to spread of the high-wheel (ordinary) cycle there was a proliferation of tricycle construction and use, in which the carrier tricycle, Norcliffe argues, building on his earlier (2001) work, represented the novelty of modernity itself. That the carrying capacity of the novel designs could apply to either goods or passengers alerts us to another layer in the working cycle story and one that has been and remains vitally important. The passenger-carrying cycle – in its various passenger rickshaw forms – is almost certainly the most numerous type of working cycle in existence today. Rickshaws, boda boda (bicycle taxis) and other passenger carrying cycles demand their own history and will have to remain largely outside the scope of this chapter (see *Transfers* (2013) 3(3) "Special Section on Rickshaws" for recent work).

The development of the "safety" bicycle in the late 1880s did not displace existing tricycle designs but offered new possibilities for tricycle layout and construction. Further, the safety bicycle principle (in which indirect drive allows for smaller wheels and a seating position nearer to the ground) offered new possibilities for the construction of carrier bicycles. For the manufacturer, the potential of practical uses for the cycle provided a second, expanding market. The solo bicycle of the 1890s was not immediately conceived of as a practical utility transport vehicle (Clyde, 1895). It was a superb design for the leisure of gentlemen and ladies and for the pursuit of sporting endeavour, but its employment by workers who would have to carry the tools of their trade required degrees of adaptation. More importantly, the sheer price of cycles kept them out of reach of most British workers in the 1890s except as a transport provided by their employers (Cox, 2015). Elsewhere, where cycle prices were relatively lower, *The Wheel and Cycle Trader* (USA, 19 February 1897) could report that their

> observer is surprised to see the general use which the bicycle has found amongst the mechanics in that northern country [Denmark]. It is made to serve as a valuable tool in the furtherance of various trades and masons, bricklayers, carpenters and such can be seen speeding along the streets.

It was therefore at employers that specifically built carrier cycles (and trailers, produced during the same period) were aimed – especially since they cost twice the price of a standard bicycle.

The economic division between the middle classes (about 25–33% of the population) who could afford servants to run the domestic household and those employed by them to do so, shaped the pattern of late Victorian retail. Although only some 10% of workers were in service by 1900, the gulf between workers' wages and those of the middle classes enabled the boom in consumer goods in the latter years of the nineteenth century as a form of conspicuous consumption (Veblen, 1899). The bicycle itself was one of the beneficiaries of the cyclical boom–bust of rapidly changing fashions, particularly between 1896 and 1898. The distinction between the sale of items of fashion and discretionary purchases and the retail and distribution of household necessities mimicked the class distinctions of the household divisions of labour. The middle-class woman might be desirous of time to spend in a fashionable department store, but it would be a task for the maidservant to arrange for the purchase of the mundane items of grocery that she or the cook would be preparing.

Prior to the adoption of any form of self-service, the Victorian retailer, even of the most everyday goods, was a salesperson mediating between the customer and the object. As mediator, the retailer would also usually be expected to deliver as well as supply. And it was in this space that the working bicycle was offered as a means to increase efficiency. Two alternatives were available: animal traction delivery services by cart or wagon, or handcart. The carrier cycle not only offered the symbolic imagery of modernity, but also practical advantages. It could carry as much as a handcart but cover significantly more distance in the same time. Although providing less carrying capacity than animal traction, there were no constant running costs and it could easily be left unattended or unused (and unfed).

It is not surprising therefore that we see the early appearance of what were to become the iconic uses of delivery cycles – for butchers, bakers and grocers – even at this early stage. Characteristic of the design of solo bicycles around the turn of the century was the gradual reduction of diversity and the production of similar models from year to year (Oddy, 2007). For cycles intended for trade purposes, however, while yearly innovation is absent, the variety of designs only seems to have multiplied as responses to the problem of cargo carriage produced an increasing variety of ever more specialized solutions.

It is also worth noting that the bicycle was an international trade commodity. While localized production and innovation is clear in the pages of trade journals, so too is the constant exchange of ideas and news from markets around the globe (see, for examples *The Wheel and Cycling Trade Review* and the *Referee and Cycle Trader* (both USA) and *Kaleidescop* (Germany)). Consequently, news of new designs and developments travelled rapidly and manufacturers constantly looked for market opportunities. Perhaps one of the most striking examples is the export of Jin Riksha (hand-drawn rickshaws) from the USA to Japan in the late 1890s where American manufacturers took advantage of the current underdevelopment of Japanese production facilities (*The Wheel and Cycle Trader*, 12 October, 1899, p. 16). One surprising – but also obvious – development of cargo bikes for goods distribution was those built to carry bicycles themselves. Cycle retailers in both the USA and Germany could purchase carrier tricycles for the express purpose of carrying bicycles.

Cycle use spread to the masses at different times in different European locations, as price controls on cycle sales and working wages shifted relative to one another (Cox, 2015). Nevertheless by the end of the 1920s bicycles had become the most numerous vehicles on the roads, and provided autonomous and independent mobility to ever widening classes of people. Despite changes in patterns of physical mobility and against the background of economic depression and widespread un-employment, patterns in general retailing and the transport of goods to the customer were relatively unchanged. At the upper end of the retail business, stores such as Harrods employed fleets of electric delivery vehicles to provide final distribution of customer purchases. Initially using vehicles purchased from the USA, between 1936 and 1939 they built a fleet of sixty vehicles to their own specification. For the ordinary vendor of provisions, on the other hand, a simple bicycle provided a far more realistic means to distribute (relatively) low-bulk goods. Cargo bikes in many forms provided a means for the efficient reproduction of capital and the growth of the city (Bonham & Cox, 2010). In other European nations, cargo bikes were similarly used. In Germany, under National Socialism, cycle companies (as well as providing cycles specifically designed with party insignia to indicate one's loyalty) listed carrier cycles as part of their standard ranges. Even though the catalogues of (for example) Phänomen-Werke Gustave Hiller Ag from 1934 and 1936 show very little design variation from the 1908 range, they continued to include a trade bike in their range of eight models (including one motorcycle). Alongside the general catalogue, the carrier cycle was described in a separate brochure, indicative perhaps of the different clientele for whom it was intended. Its unique selling point was the design of a front carrier with an integral stand, (i.e. under the centre of the load, and the basket could be arranged in three different positions providing different load-carrying options from a 52 x 34 x 10 cm high basket to a 52 x 46 cm flatbed. The latter would be an obvious option for goods transported already presented loaded on trays, for example bakery and patisserie deliveries. Photographic records demonstrate the ubiquity of working cycles in the Netherlands and Denmark, and a majority of general cycle manufacturers list at least one model especially strengthened for portage purposes, as well as there being a number of forms specializing exclusively in working cycle production, in a wide range of specialized designs.

In France, the newspaper industry – which extensively used cycle sport to sell newspapers – also employed specially built or adapted cycles for paper distribution. In keeping with the sponsorship of racing, successive newspapers ran a Critérium de Porteurs de Journaux and a Championnat des Triporteurs. In these events the newspaper delivery riders raced cargo tricycles loaded with up to 40 kg of ballast (Metz, n.d.). These races started in 1895, reached a heyday during the 1930s and continued on until the 1960s, although steadily decreasing in importance. Triporteurs, carrier tricycles with two wheels at the front creating a space for cargo, had been produced since the turn of the century (see e.g. Nöll, 2011, p. 171) and were in widespread manufacture during the 1920s. The French firm of Blotto, in common with others, also produced motorized versions, so fulfilling the niche of micro-van. From these earlier celebrations of utility, we can see the declining status of the triporteur in popular culture, in France at least, by the two films of Darry Cowl (*Le Triporteur* [1957] and *Robinson et le Triporteur* [1959]) in which the rider of the local delivery cycle is a figure of comic ridicule, rather mocked and looked down on. The machine has become a signifier of obsolescence.

Outside of European cities – the metropolitan centres of empires – the practical working cycle underwent its most profound and lasting development with the advent of the cycle-rickshaw. Hand-drawn rickshaws had become ubiquitous means for transporting goods and passengers in cities across East Asia since their inception in the 1860s (Gallagher, 1992). Combining the transport body of a hand-drawn rickshaw with the drive and steering of a cycle, the cycle rickshaw provided yet another variation of working tricycle design and one which was almost synonymous with Asian urban mobility by the latter part of the twentieth century. Passenger rickshaw design varies regionally (Wheeler & I'Anson 1998), some designs echoing passenger tricycles of the 1890s rather than the 1930s model. Whatever their design, their capacity to carry considerable loads, whether human passengers or cargo, allows rickshaws greater penetration into retail distribution, carrying both product and customer. They serve their delivery purposes not only from store to home but at most stages of the distribution cycle. (Although passenger-carrying cycles and trailers have been built sporadically since the 1890s, passenger traffic by bicycle remained almost entirely absent in twentieth-century Europe, the only examples found so far being in photographs of the Warsaw ghetto in 1941/2, Bundesarchive, Berlin).

After 1945

We have suggested above that the style of working cycles in local use corresponds to the structure of the retail sector. In turn, this is further connected to patterns of urbanization and industrialization, income distributions and household compositions, including gender roles in relation to domesticity and labour markets. Further complexity can be added to this mix when we consider national variations in cultural histories and associations of cycle use with social class and social status. In the rapid changes of post-war Europe through the 1950s and 1960s, it is not surprising that we also see considerable changes in the use of working bikes. Although parallel to the decline of cycle use for personal transport, we suggest that the reasons for the decline of working cycles are not quite the same.

The impact of fuel restrictions during the Second World War had served to consolidate the centrality of the bicycle as a prime utility vehicle, not simply for personal transport, but for the continued supply of smaller goods in local areas. Yet the very ordinariness of delivery cycles accounts for their near invisibility in historical accounts. Working cycles, used as trade vehicles, however, were not just subject to the general decline in social value of the bicycle from the 1950s onwards, but victims also of profound changes to goods distribution from the very late 1950s through to the 1970s: part of the emergence of new forms of consumer society and of transformations in retailing. Firstly, during this period there are transformations in the structure of middle-class households. Domestic service almost entirely disappears and in its place, married women's roles became more firmly identified with householding and domestic responsibility (Johnson & Lloyd, 2004; Freeman, 2004). This resulted in a change in the purchaser: the domestic householder was now directly concerned with purchase of everyday necessities.

For retailers, the growth of direct payment and self-service reshaped the shopping experience. The purchaser no longer had to speak first to a salesperson, who would then issue a chit for goods which would have to be taken to a separate payments desk (or simply put on account). The traditional separation between act of purchase and the actual acquisition of the goods by the purchaser made delivery services a logical extension of the service function of the supplier. Although most familiar as a system in department stores, this same system was used even in small village shops. Self-service systems allowing direct contact between the customer and the goods, together with increasing volumes of direct cash transactions (rather than operating on account) allowed the retailer to cede responsibility for goods at the point of sale direct to the customer. Indeed, the point of sale moves into the store, rather than being a protracted process of accounts held with regular delivery and payment in an ongoing relationship between localized customers and goods suppliers. Self-service and direct payment shifted primary responsibility for the transport of purchases from the retailer to the customer/consumer.

In turn, the growth of motorized mobility, first by motorcycle and scooter and later by private cars, facilitated growth in the radius of travel available, allowing customers to choose from a greater range of locations for shopping and breaking the direct link with sole local suppliers. This assisted the breakdown of regular, locally dependent relationships necessary for the success of a delivery business. One important cause of this was the profound drop in energy costs relative to wages that occurred across Europe during the 1950s (Pfister, 1998). By 1969 in the United Kingdom, 50% of households had access to a car, and this increased mobility and carrying capacity provided the spaces for the symbiotic expansion of the supermarket. Increases in married women's employment levels during the 1970s also helped support the logic of the supermarket and its ability to consolidate shopping for necessities into a single transaction. The private car provided a means to easily transport the larger volumes of goods resulting from this weekly grocery-shopping trip. By the mid 1970s, the cargo bike as a means of goods distribution was all but extinct and with the loss of trade sales went most of the few remaining independent manufacturers of tradesman's and carrier cycles in the UK (for example the Leonard Gundle Motor Co. Ltd which closed in 1974), most others having disappeared in the consolidations of the cycle industry in the 1960s although Raleigh continued production until the 1970s (Rosen, 2003).

The Cargo Bike is Dead, Long Live the Cargo Bike

Almost as soon as the working cycle as a function of trade had died, it was to be reborn with a subtly different identity. The bicycle re-emerged in Europe in the 1970s as both practical transport and, more importantly for our case here, as a symbol of critical social values and of a growing environmental consciousness (Rosen, 2002; Horton, 2006; Stoffers & Cox, 2010). As relatively simple machines, bicycles have considerable longevity, especially those built for robustness. Ending commercial production did not mean their disappearance. Similarly, they are relatively easy vehicles to construct on a small scale with only basic tooling and metalworking skills. This made bikes of all sorts ideal components of counter-cultures, especially those encompassing concepts of autonomy and those critical of the car-dominance and its impact on both urban and rural life.

To claim the bicycle as primary practical transport in northern Europe in the 1970s (whether at individual or at state level) was to pass comment on the increasing dominance of private motor traffic. It is not surprising that we see new designs of cargo-practical carrier cycles and trailers made and distributed through counter-cultural networks and communities. Most famous are the Christiana bikes first built in

1976. But at the same time, in Uden (Netherlands) old carrier bikes were being rehabilitated and celebrated in a Bak-en Transportfietsenrace (in its seventh edition by 1982). Manufacture for trade may have disappeared but the practicality of personal ownership of bicycles specifically built with load-carrying in mind, especially those items or volumes of goods not easily accommodated on a conventional solo bicycle, has an obvious appeal for those who choose not to use a private car. As the promotion of alternatives to urban car use accelerated in the 1980s and 1990s, so too load-carrying cycles – cargo bikes of all styles – became a clear, specialist niche. Modern cargo bikes provide a means by which their users can participate in societies characterized by systems of automobility, but without necessarily participating in an automotive lifestyle.

The cargo bike had a role in the formation of twentieth-century consumer capitalism, as a means of distribution of consumer products. Its place disappeared as the retail trade outsourced final distribution to the customer – part of the customer's transitions to consumer, enabled by the growth of private motor transport. The cargo bike re-emerged as a counter-cultural alternative to the car, enabling continued participation in societies restructured by automobility (Alvord, 2000; Urry, 2004). As recognition of the unsustainability, impracticability and undesirability of accommodating universal urban private motoring (and the rebuilding of cities necessary to facilitate this) has spread, so what was once the basis of a marginal critique has been translated into mainstream policy for many European cities. Thus the cargo bike re-emerges as an obvious and logical household transport option regardless of its recent counter-cultural heritage where discourses of sustainable transport policy have traction.

The discussion of the changing identity and fortunes of the working cycle in Europe should not blind us to its very different histories elsewhere around the globe. Although beyond the scope of this chapter, it is clear that the twentieth century narrative of the working bike as a function of the organization of trade should produce different histories outside of the geographical limits of this study. Fieldwork studies in Rio de Janeiro demonstrate that, despite being almost invisible from official statistics, locally produced cycles of a wide range of designs continue to be used for a range of goods delivery services, carrying items as large as mattresses. Cycles also serve the role of mobile retail units, bringing goods to the customer on the street and selling items as diverse as meat and jewellery. The sale of ice cream and other goods from mobile refrigerators and freezers mounted on tricycles is not limited to European history. Street traders across the globe use bicycles as mobile bases for business, demonstrating adaptations and innovations to suit their particular needs. For some retailers today, the use of the bicycle is a signifier of green credentials or of a commitment to broader social values, while for others it may simply provide an innovative sales pitch and talking point to increase brand recognition.

Some European delivery services, particularly those involved in carriage of mail and the couriering of other small packaged goods have provided continuous patterns of cycle use and kept carrier cycles in the public eye. Post offices are perhaps one of the strongest examples, although the Royal Mail here in the UK is perhaps atypical in phasing out bicycle postal deliveries in 2014, bucking the trend of other delivery services. Although disappearing from view, working bicycles and tricycles of all types have proved remarkably resilient and even when subject to legislative bans (for example, in Jakarta) have continued to be used. There is considerable scope for a lot more detailed research in this area where a long past impacts upon a mutable present.

Over 100 years from the first generation of cargo bike designs, the end of the twentieth century and the early years of the twenty-first have seen a flourishing of European cargo bike design and production. Initially, however, these were characterized by a reverse relationship to retail and the reproduction of capital. The trade bike prospered in the first half of the twentieth century as it offered increased efficiency for delivery services over its alternatives (handcart, horse or motor traction). For its advocates at the end of the twentieth century, the working cycle began to spread as an item of domestic ownership. In increasing variety of designs, carrier bicycles and tricycles have become iconic in the promotion of cycle-friendly cities. However, since the mid 2000s, a new generation of cargo bikes has begun to appear as a vital element in commercial use once more. It is to this resurgence – a third phase of cargo bike use – that we now turn our attention.

The Re-Invention of the Commercial Cargo Bike

The advent of the digital economy, just-in-time delivery systems and rapid rises in energy costs in the transport sector have brought an almost unprecedented importance to logistics for all sorts of commercial activities, not just retail. For urban deliveries, the first and last mile poses major problems of expense and congestion. Since most goods, regardless of weight, reach their final destination in city centres in motorized cars, vans and trucks logistic companies have to fight for limited space. Further, large trucks and lorries are becoming unpopular within urban areas among both policy makers and politicians concerned not only with congestion, pollution and wear and tear on roads but for their disproportionate involvement in collisions (Dutch Institute for Road Safety Research, 2009) and cyclist fatalities (Schoon et al., 2008). Additionally, there are significant pressures arising from the need to take the sustainability agenda seriously, especially in light of CO_2 emissions in the transport sector. Consequently, cities are increasingly looking towards reducing freight traffic within cities and urban areas. City centres are frequently being closed off to delivery vans, wholly or at particular times of day. Vehicles may also be subject to congestion charges or other regulations which add significant economic burdens on urban logistics.

These transformations of the urban environment make the operation of working cycles an increasingly attractive commercial option once more, whether for dedicated logistics operators, or for other delivery options for individual or corporate retailers. DHL Netherlands reported saving €430,000 per year after replacing thirty-three trucks with thirty-three cargo bikes. Since July 2012, the European Cycle Logistics Federation (ECLF) has brought together organizations from advocacy and commercial sectors, seeking to expand the commercial use of cargo bikes in European cities as a means both to combat congestion and to provide "green credentials with zero carbon emissions" (www.ecf.com/projects/cyclelogistics-2/). The ECLF was officially incorporated in 2014 (http://federation. cyclelogistics.eu/) and counted over 150 members. It was created under the auspices of the CycleLogistics project, (http://www.cyclelogistics.eu/) co-funded by the EU Intelligent Energy – Europe Programme, from 2011 to 2014. The project promoted the use of cargo bikes for the movement of goods in EU cities. The project team calculated that 51% of logistics trips made in EU cities with motor vehicles could be replaced by cycle trips. Other projections showed that 25% of commercial deliveries could easily be shifted to cycles. This potential was one reason why EU funding was forthcoming for a new project.

Running from 2014 to 2017, CycleLogistics Ahead (www.cyclelogistics.eu/) targets business and municipal sectors as potential new users of cargo cycles in a range of applications where current motor vehicle use is deemed unwarranted. A number of similar projects are also in action to explore the potential of new electric vehicle, including pedelec cycle-based delivery and distribution systems, again echoing the restructuring of the commercial mobility landscape a century ago.

What we see is a very rapid transformation of a single technology from the icon of a cultural critique (a cachet which it still possesses, at least in part, for many users) to the emblem of a more efficient city. The economic case for the use of working cycles for urban distribution and delivery services is strong. Just as cycle (and motorcycle) messenger services have provided specialist delivery services through the second half of the twentieth century, the incorporation of cargo-carrying cycles to these kinds of operations enables the expansion of these services to provide a constant flow of deliveries through urban spaces, unimpeded by many of the restrictions that hinder conventional motor vehicles. A further element of the digital economy to have major impact on retailing is the growth in online shopping. Expanding volumes of home deliveries, especially in small items, coupled with market liberalization of postal systems, leads to heightened competitiveness, and services that offer any kind of marginal advantage are increasingly attractive.

Production of cargo bikes is now no longer just the domain of small-scale local manufacture. The German Chancellor Angela Merkel visited the 2013 Eurobike tradefair and posed with a cargo bike produced by Accell, a major cycle producer. New product design enables contemporary cargo bikes with three or four wheels to carry considerable loads, up to 250 kg. Reihle (2012) documented six different models on the retail market that claim maximum payloads of 400 kg. The potential of both smaller and larger capacity cargo bikes is now being explored in relation to new logistical models for freight distribution, using peri-urban hubs for large-scale drop-offs, the hubs then acting as bases for localized distribution networks. Systems approaches to logistical efficiency, with cargo bikes as an integral part of the network, offer considerable gains not just in environmental sustainability, but in making cities places for people, not motor vehicles.

Conclusions

An extremely broad range of factors has shaped the changing fortunes of the working bicycle, most of which are extrinsic to the machine. Household patterns and the division of domestic labour has been crucial. The availability of independent mobility, relative fuel costs, retailers' own prioritizations (bottom line versus USP [Unique Selling Point]) and the state of class relations between retailer and customer have all played parts.

At its simplest, the story of European working cycles is a story of the role of the commerce they have served. As patterns of retail and distribution have changed, so the fortunes of commercially operated bicycles have risen and fallen according to their location within a bigger picture. Their re-emergence and re-manufacture by independent innovators in the late 1970s is a notable irregularity, but a logical corollary of renewed emphasis on cycles as transport in a period when the mainstream cycle industry had largely relegated cycles to a role as leisure products. The sheer longevity of many trade bicycles also contributes to their persistence in private ownership, and the continued presence of working bikes in key roles, even when invisible in other uses, enabled them to maintain a presence in the imagination.

If we consider the cargo bike as a cultural phenomenon, we can see a number of distinct phase changes in its perceptions and place. The same basic object can be read as a signifier, changing its meaning for different social groups over time as both users and contexts change. At the end of the 1890s, as Norcliffe demonstrates, the cargo bike appears as a symbol of modernity. General bicycle manufacturers' catalogues include them within their main body, as an indicator of their versatility and comprehensiveness. As the ubiquity of the bicycle was embedded in the

147

everyday life of inter-war Europe, specialist manufacturers of carrier cycles grew to meet the diverse needs of businesses alongside the offerings of major companies. Because unremarkable, like the everyday bicycle for transport, it had become transparent to the point of invisibility. Towards the end of the 1950s, not only was it no longer a signifier of modernity, but increasingly functionally redundant as delivery services were abandoned in place of self-service and direct sales.

But no sooner had increasing mobility throughout the general population signalled the demise of commercial retail delivery services, than counter-cultural critiques of that motorized mobility – its impact and implications – created new spaces for cargo bikes. Cargo bikes and trailers became symbolic of new possibilities of mobile life, especially urban mobility. In the changing contexts of urban development policy, they move from signifiers of alternative lifestyles to symbols of rational choice. It is in this last mode that the cargo bike wheel turns full circle, as the economic rationality of carrier cycles as a logical choice for business makes them once more a desirable commodity. This is not only in simple monetary economic terms, but also as indicators of business commitment to improving urban life. Once again they become symbols of a new progressivism for more sustainable futures.

References

Alvord, K. (2000). *Divorce your Car! Ending the Love Affair with the Automobile*. Gabrioloa Island, BC, Canada: New Society Publishers.

Bonham, J., & Cox, P. (2010). The Disruptive Traveller? A Foucauldian Analysis of Cycleways. *Road and Transport Research 19*(2), 42–53.

Bowlby, R. (2001). *Carried Away: The Invention of Modern Shopping*. New York, NY: Columbia University Press.

Burr, T. (2012). National Market Communities: Bicycle Use and Civil Society in France and the United States 1867–1910. *Consumption Markets and Culture, 15*(1), 63–85.

Clyde, H. (1895). *Pleasure-Cycling*. Boston, USA: Little, Brown and Company.

Cox, P. (2015). Towards a Better Understanding of Bicycles as Transport. In M. Moraglio & K. Kopper (eds.), *The Organization of Transport: A History of Users, Industry, and Public Policy* (pp. 49–67). New York: Routledge.

Dutch Institute for Road Safety Research. (2009). http://www.swov.nl/rapport/Factsheets/UK/FS_Blind_spot_crashes.pdf

Edwards, J.B., McKinnon, A.C., & Cullinane, S.L. (2009). *Carbon Auditing the 'Last Mile': Modelling the Environmental Impacts of Conventional and Online Non-Food Shopping*. Paper for Logistics Research Centre, School of Management and Languages. Heriot-Watt University. Retrieved from: www.sml. hw.ac.uk/logistics & www.greenlogistics.org.uk

Francks, P., & Hunter, J. (eds.) (2012). *The Historical Consumer: Consumption and Everyday Life in Japan, 1850–2000*. Basingstoke, UK: Palgrave Macmillan.

Freeman, J. (2004).*The Making of the Modern Kitchen: A Cultural History*. Oxford, UK: Berg.

Gallagher, R. (1992). *The Rickshaws of Bangladesh*. Dhaka, Bangladesh: The University Press.

Graham, K. (2008). *Gone to the Shops: Shopping in Victorian England*. Westport, CT: Praeger.

Hadland, T., & Lessing, H.-E. (2014). *Bicycle Design: An Illustrated History*. Cambridge, MA: MIT Press.

Horton, D. (2006). Environmentalism and the Bicycle. *Environmental Politics, 15*(1), 41–58.

Illustrierte Zeitung (Leipzig), No. 1357. 3 July 1869 (Volume 53), p. 15. In The Deutsches Museum Photographic Archives, File 220, BN 113843.

"Jap Carriages" (1899). *The Wheel and Cycle Trader*, 12 October, p. 16.

Johnson, L., & Lloyd, J. (2004). *Sentenced to Everyday Life: Feminism and the Housewife*. Oxford: Berg.

Metz, J. (n.d.). www.blackbirdsf.org/courierracing [accessed 24 March 2008].

Miles, S. (2012). The Neoliberal City and the Pro-Active Complicity of the Citizen Consumer. *Journal of Consumer Culture, 12*, 216–230. doi: 10.1177/1469540512446881.

Miller, D., Jackson, P., Thrift, N., Holbrook, B., & Rowlands, M. (1998). *Shopping, Place and Identity*. London, UK: Routledge.

Nöll, J. (2011). *Opel Fahrräder. Fünf Jahrzehnte Fahrradbau in Rüsselheim*. Bielefeld, Germany: Delius Klasing.

Norcliffe, G. (2001). *The Ride to Modernity: The Bicycle in Canada 1869–1900*. Toronto, Canada: University of Toronto Press.

Norcliffe, G. (2011). Neoliberal Mobility and its Discontents: Working Tricycles in China's Cities, *City, Culture and Society,* 2(4), 235–242. http://dx.doi.org/10.1016/j.ccs.2011.11.006.

Oddy, N. (2007). The Flaneur on Wheels? In D. Horton, P. Rosen, & P. Cox (eds.), *Cycling & Society* (pp. 25–46). Aldershot, UK: Ashgate Publishing.

Pfister, C. (1998). The 'Syndrome of the 1950s' in Switzerland. Cheap Energy, Mass Consumption, and the Environment. In S. Strasser, C. McGovern, & M. Judt (eds.), *Getting and Spending, European and American Consumer Societies in the Twentieth Century* (pp. 359–377). New York: Cambridge University Press.

Reihle, E.-B. (2012). *Das Lastenfahrrad als Transportmittel fur Stadtischen Wirtschaftsverkehr* [Cargo bikes as transportation vehicles for urban freight traffic] Dortmund, Germany: Faculty of Spatial Planning, TU Dortmund University, DLR Institute of Transport Research.

Rosen, P. (2002). *Up the Vélorution: Appropriating the Bicycle and the Politics of Technology* [SATSU Working paper N24 2002]. Science & Technology Studies Unit, University of York, UK.

Rosen, P. (2003). *Framing Production: Sociotechnical Change in the British Bicycle Industry.* Cambridge, MA: MIT Press.

Schoon, C., Doumen, M., & de Bruin, D. (2008). The Circumstances of Blind Spot Crashes and Short- and Long-Term Measures. R-2008-11A en R-2008-11B. Leidschendam, Netherlands: SWOV.

Stoffers, M., & Cox, P. (2010). Beyond Technology: The Bicycle Renaissance as a Case in the History of Mobility. Paper presented to Mobility and the Environment Workshop at the Rachel Carson Center for Environment and Society, Munich, 3–5 June 2010.

Strasser, S., McGovern, C., & Judt, M. (eds.). *Getting and Spending, European and American Consumer Societies in the Twentieth Century* (pp. 359–377). New York: Cambridge University Press.

Urry, J. (2004) The "System" of Automobility, *Theory, Culture and Society,* 21 (4/5), 25–39.

Veblen, T. (1899). *The Theory of the Leisure Class: An Economic Study of Institutions.* New York: Macmillan.

Wheeler, T., & I'Anson, R. (1998). *Chasing Rickshaws.* Hawthorn, Australia: Lonely Planet Publications.

CHAPTER 7

RANDONNEURSHIP – A MODERN CYCLING CONSTRUCTION

Heike Bunte

Introduction

Modern randonneuring – organized cycling over very long distances – has been practised for more than 100 years. Statistical data on the number of participants and their speeds has been gathered since 1891 for the world's largest endurance event in cycling, the renowned Paris-Brest-Paris run (Déon, 1997). This marathon of 1,230 km and others of lesser length are known as "brevets" (French for examination) or randonnées and participants are called randonneurs (French for rambler). Today's participants are neither professionals nor have they had anything like a professional sports career. On the contrary, they are ordinary people in everyday life (Voss, 1991), most of them normally employed. To be able to accomplish the supreme discipline of Paris-Brest-Paris within the given ninety-hour time limit, participants have to qualify first, riding recognized tests of 200, 300, 400 and 600 km before the final brevet (randonneuring distances are always calculated in kilometres, even in the British club, Audax UK).

This chapter examines the specific subculture of these events and their riders, seeking to look more closely at what might appear on the surface to be an extraordinary, even somewhat ludicrous activity. What measures do randonneurs take to ensure that they cross the finishing line within the time limits set, and reliant solely on their own muscle power? Should they go faster and stop longer, or ride at a slower road average and stop less frequently. A maximum time limit of 13 hours for 200 km provides a total average of somewhat more than 15 km/h (9 mph), a velocity which allows enough time for breaks at a speed

152

that can be called "relaxed" (for regulations, see http://www.audax-randonneure.de). Minimum time limits are also enforced in order to prevent racing. How do participants adjust their athletic bodies and sporting activities, and what does constant, long-term and monotonous pedalling mean (Gressmann, 1995) when cycle sport is notorious for speed and transient experience? How does the randonneur master the scale of the undertaking, and how do they find out which modes of interaction with others en route are most useful, in particular in the interplay between cooperative and competitive relations, when at the same time the cycling rules prescribe that the randonneur overcomes the large distances and brevets on their own whenever this is possible?

Although randonneuring, or Audax riding as it is sometimes known, is an international phenomenon, this chapter concentrates on a study of German randonneurs, drawing from research conducted during a much larger previous study (Bunte, 2009). Participants in different contexts have created unique cultures of randonneuring, such that an event in one nation is still recognizable as a brevet to a rider from another, but may have distinctive local characteristics. Similarly amateur leisure (racing) events are also an international phenomenon, prompting considerable international travel. Again this study concentrates primarily on evidence from the German context.

Cycling accelerates human motion. Compared to walking and running, it allows us to travel greater distances in less time. In comparison with other modes of transport, such as car or coach, it still solely relies on the limits of human muscle power, but this lower speed allows more time for interaction and social communication. Growing participation rates, and the changing interactions and ways of seeing prompted by these, coupled with increasing rates of technological change suggest that these forms of cycling involve two elements of acceleration: technical and social. Change is accelerated and heightened in both these spheres. In particular, current leisure cycle sport projects an image of progress, of modernity, and is increasingly geared towards and connected with images of professional sports. By contrast randonneuring rather sees itself (and depicts itself), as a distinctly "decelerated" variety of cycling, stressing continuity rather than innovation. Despite tremendous engineering enhancements since the advent of this long-distance discipline, average randonneur speeds have not significantly increased (Pooch, 2008). Indeed, the regulations governing participants today ensure that they cannot increase beyond a pre-set limit.

Cycling as a system of motion takes various forms (Leibbrand, 2008; Oddy, 2007; Schenkel, 2008; Lüders, 1925). We can observe, as others in this volume do, that these are profoundly diverse: from the quotidian journey of unremarkable activity and content, through the joyful play of children, to highly trained athletic activity. The subject of this chapter – randonneuring – shows both continuity and contrast with other, more familiar forms of ambitious leisure cycling, touring and racing (Lindner, 2005). In particular, when considering cycling not for its capacity as travel (moving the body from a to b), but as a form of bodily motion, randonneuring creates a sequence of body movements that resemble the repetitive, monotonous motion of a machine, characterized by consistency, not changing with the varying flow of a tour or a race (Ückert, 2004). What prompts people to engage in activities that substantially exceed what is generally understood as reasonable physical activity in any sport (Neumann et al., 1999)? Before examining randonneuring in detail it is useful to consider another form of riding that requires a high degree of bodily subjugation.

Sportive Riding as Disciplined Subordination

With the growing interest in cycle sport, especially linked to high profile sporting heroes (and anti-heroes), more and more leisure cyclists have ventured on events over distances of up to 180 km over the last decades in order to vent their racing aspirations. With average minimum speeds of 30 km/h and maximum speeds well above 35 km/h these leisure (racing) cyclists ride between 6,000 and 8,000 km per year thus obviously coping brilliantly with the challenge of acceleration. At this pace, 180 km means cyclists are spending five to six hours in the saddle. Such distances and speeds are no longer extraordinary for leisure cyclists (Friel, 2007). This form of leisure cycling therefore represents short-term activities of athletic bodies (Shilling 2003): they are characterized by group riding, quick changes of leader on the road and a strict hierarchy depending on the individual performance (Lindner, 2005). This scenario reminds us of the so-called domestiques, whose only task in professional cycle sport is to assist the team leader to the finish line, to let the protected one draft behind to conserve energy, so that they can give their all in the last miles and be celebrated as glorious heroes.

The whirring and clicking of race machines and the noise of a group of racers rushing past is well known not only during pro events (Moll, 2000), but also during the so-called "open" or citizen races. Sports organizers cater for ever-growing numbers of leisure sportsmen and women such that a new class of event, known in English as sportive riding, has proliferated. Larger events become media phenomena. In responses to the consumer needs of recreational athletes, a new shape of cycling is being formed. This is not traditional cycle racing, which continues to be organized within cycling clubs and national federations, but a parallel world of professionally organized events run on a commercial basis. It is accompanied by the phenomenon that amateur cyclists are acting almost like their professional counterparts, including riding in a peloton (a mass group) to take advantage of the shielding effect and using the *wedel* technique while stationary (changing the direction of the bike using only the feet) (http://www.vattenfall-cyclassics.de).

Riding in a bunch allows slipstreaming and taking turns in the front saves energy for covering longer distances. This type of cycling requires a precisely timed choreography in which the actors have internalized the timed cycle of riding in front. The cyclists are tightly packed – always trying to stay closely behind one another. Each millimetre of distance that is lost between the wheels of the machines results in poorer aerodynamics (Pooch, 2009). Individual failure to "hold the wheel" [i.e. stay tightly behind the cycle in front of you] puts the whole group at a disadvantage. Worse, momentary loss of control – a touch of wheels, for example – can lead to mass crashes. These behaviours must be learned, skills practised that require hours of dedication – and the leisure time in which to follow these pursuits. For newer riders without the advantage of the longer socialization processes of traditional club riding and racing, these can be difficult skills. Amateur cyclists' behaviour in these events emulates the conduct of professional racing. They sweep past, demonstrating how they are able to handle their machines with the greatest of ease. Riding en masse as a peloton, they mimetically illustrate enormous physical control over their bikes. Their sports clothing is turned into advertising hoardings replicating the sponsorship of professionals. They are equipped with measuring instruments, such as heart-rate monitors, cadence meters, even power meters, together with GPS navigation devices and bicycle computers. These are often expensive articles used in professional competitive sports. There is often little difference anymore between recreational cyclists with their equipment and their technically upgraded and well-equipped machines and the actors of the professional racing teams. Indeed, the advent of mass-produced carbon-fibre frames has meant that any amateur rider who can afford it can ride exactly the same machine as the professionals, even more so than in the days of steel frames, when a mass market maker's badge might well conceal a bespoke frame. But this is an expensive pastime when pursued in this manner, not simply for the financial cost of the latest equipment, but also in the high time costs required.

The attempts of leisure sports to imitate professional sports have shown themselves in the provision of finishers' medals and even in the "broom wagon" that sweeps up riders who have given up due to injury, fatigue or breakage. Similarly, use of doping-related substances, has become a big issue in recreational cycling in Germany. The Drug Control Officer of the Federal Government underlined several legal initiatives in her report (Die Drogenbeauftragte der Bundesregierung, 2011, p. 47). In short, the leisure racing cyclists epitomize subordination to a very specific set of ideals, standards and practices. The body is pushed to its physical limit for the duration of the activity.

Of course, this is not true for all sportive events, and in the UK in particular, where they cater for larger numbers of relatively novice riders, events are frequently graded to encourage participation and to allow for shorter distances and lower speeds for some participants.

Randonneuring as Work-Oriented Long-Distance Cycling

Overall, long distance cycling is gaining in popularity (Déon 1997). Riders wish to face the physical and mental challenge of bike riding to the extreme (Bette, 2004). In total contrast to the common subordination and musculature of the enthusiastic shorter-distance, higher-speed cyclists, randonneuring has a more refined attitude and represents itself as a highly individualized, singular performance (Schröder, 2000). Randonneuring requires a physical endurance beyond that found in more commonly accepted and acknowledged recreational sport interests. These riders neither make a profession of their adventurous extreme sport, nor are they specially born to this kind of activity. On the contrary, during the research for this study, I came across a number of men, aged 40 or over, most of whom, having been told by their doctors to take more exercise (such as swimming, running or cycling), chose cycling. Some of these later became randonneurs. Yet randonneuring provides a very different frame of reference to other forms of ambitious leisure cycling – race oriented or not. They do not ride at their physical limits at maximum pace. Instead, bodily output is moderated while at the same time pushed to test limits of endurance. Riders typically cover distances of 10,000 to 16,000 km per year, although this may be much higher. In a similar related test of endurance, organized brevets will often seek to encompass the maximum amount of climbing possible in the course of their distance. In English, such terrain is euphemistically referred to as "scenic".

The international Randonneur or Audax Clubs (from the Latin, meaning audacity, boldness, spirit of adventure), as they name themselves, offer official brevets: recognized rides. The brevets follow strict rules that define the distance to be ridden. Provision and time organization are in the hands of the randonneurs. There are both permanent routes, ridden any time at the rider's discretion, and events which take place on a given day, organized by club members themselves, where all participants start at the same time and place to ride the set distance. Official routes are given for the brevets and their distances. Riding these distances can be understood as modern (cycling) adventures. The randonneurs are, apart from some official checkpoints, reliant on their own provisions and power over the whole distance, even when they use technical aids, such as navigation devices.

The checkpoints also have a control function to avoid "cheating" or rule-breaking, either taking short cuts or riding faster than the set maximum speed would contravene the regulations. The start time, the arrival time at each intermediate checkpoint (which must be inside the official opening and closing time for each) and the finish time are recorded on a route card (brevet) for each randonneur so that the total time can be calculated. "Permanents" provide a truly solitary test of self will. With no intermediate checkpoints available, when riding a "permanent" route, one must collect receipts from shops or ATMs or other time stamped evidences of passing through certain locations in order to certify compliance with the regulations. The "self" sees that the rules are obeyed and is at the same time the guardian of the code of honour, since it is not just a matter of riding a sports bicycle for the sake of health or of winning a medal.

The 90-Hours (Self-) Test

Paris-Brest-Paris, run every four years, is a highlight for every randonneur: the oldest continuously run cycling event in existence. It is the self-test par excellence and has seen a steadily increasing number of participants since the 1970s. The challenge of the ride is not only the 1,230 km distance (which must be completed within the 90-hour limit) but also the approximately 10,000 m of climbing undertaken along the way. The ride, like all events, takes place on the roads in regular street traffic. Roads are not closed. The event is neither supported by substantial sponsorship nor organized by professional sports agencies. Randonneur club members, working in a volunteer capacity whenever events take place, manage the organization and check the passage of riders through controls along the route on a tight budget. The cost of entry for this and other events is also low compared with professionally organized sports events.

In 2011 a total of 5,160 participants from all over the world (42 countries) joined the event, 3,602 of them (220 of them were women) completing the route within the set maximum time limit of 90 hours. The average age of the men was 49.0 years compared to 45.4 among the women. These average ages point towards the importance of a relatively time-rich lifestyle in order to be able to participate in these events, and the long hours of riding needed to prepare. The shortest time taken in 2011 was 47 hours and 42 minutes (average speed of almost 25.8 km/h), including all breaks for eating, sleeping, breakdowns and other delays. Some riders do seek to set records (van Donselaar 2011). For example, in 1991, the American Scott Dickson finished in a time of 43 h 42 m (average 28.15 km/h); Frenchwoman Nicole Chabirand in the same year finished the "Paris-Brest et retour" in 59:43 (average 20.6 km/h).

However, the winner of the first event in 1891, Charles Terront, covered the distance in 71:16 hours (average speed 17.26 km/h) (Déon, 1997, p. 384). For most participants, a time of less than 60 hours for such a distance seems to be highly ambitious and such times account for only 6.3% of riders between 1979 and 2007 (Bunte, 2009, p. 48). The majority of randonneurs take more than 70 hours to accomplish the total distance, so that for most participants, there is little change in the time taken from its inception. The technical development of accessories and materials used that might enable higher speeds is seen rather as providing a time reserve to compensate for "troubles" that may occur during the event (getting lost, technical breakdowns, "bad" weather, etc.), and so to improve the possibility of finishing inside the set time limit. In randonneuring, "improved" technology can "neutralise" only a small share of the overall effort. The limits posed by the event are primarily on the human capacity to endure, not to achieve higher physical performances. It is also clear that the "blind faith in technology" exhibited with regard to the racing machine is less decisive in endurance events than in leisure (racing) cycling where riders train to be fast (Bunte, 2009).

Randonneurship Between Modern Adventurism and Meta-Qualification

Unconventional solutions are needed on long-distance rides. As one randonneur reported, "I needed the sun cream only for stopping the clipless pedals from creaking"(Eckstein, 2011 [author's translation]). In contrast to the sportive cycling events, where the amateur riders are served commercially formulated sports drinks and high-carbohydrate snacks at drink and food stops every 30 km along the road, the randonneur must know individually how much nutrition will be needed for a distance, where to get it and how to carry it. Although feeding and rest stations are often provided for the longest-distance organized brevets (600 km and more), riders frequently utilize all-night petrol stations or stop to buy at bakeries. Organizers anticipate the riders planning hot meals during stops at commercial outlets. The permanent event rider has no benefit of organized provision and must be entirely self-sufficient and dependent on normal commercial outlets.

Randonneurs also decide on their own how long they should sleep. Many use public spaces, such as bus shelters or bank vestibules where ATMs are housed in much of continental Europe: known by randonneurs as "*Sparkassenhotels*". These bank lobbies provide free and easily accessible accommodation (just use your ATM card) which is not only dry but also heated in winter. Other places to sleep include roadside ditches and easily accessible forest paths. Sleep duration and sleep deficit are the sole decision of the randonneur. What is appropriate for each individual rider can only be found out by trial and error.

The randonneurs will have to repair their machines on their own, even in unfavourable conditions. The most resourceful will even find a solution to fix a broken frame. The simplest repair – fixing a flat tyre – is hardly worth mentioning, and how to replace broken spokes and true a wheel, if not essential, are usually within the scope of most participants. Hence they carry far more tools than sportive riders, who – frequently – may have little more than a repair kit and pump with them. The weather, climbing hundreds of metres, and possible physical reactions to any number of external events force the randonneur to per-manently observe and understand the body–machine relation in order to be able to find ad hoc solutions for any conceivable problem.

Randonneuring demands the development of the capacity for creative improvisation within the limits of what is possible. The requirements of problem solving can be both complex and contradictory, demanding competences of the same qualities. In comparison, the requirements made of the amateur racers are less wide-ranging but much more focused: their capacity for speed. What dominates this latter type of contest is not only the extreme dependence on each other but also a strictly hierarchical top-down process in the riding structure of the group. Action is taken whatever the cost; if a rider is forced to leave the group due to poor performance, he will fall behind. The individual is "burnt out" like the domestique in professional races. In the search for speed, the individual needs to conform to the physical advantaged provided by riding as a group and is supported and advantaged as long as they keep up. In the pure endurance of the randonée, the comfort of finding one's own rhythm and riding at one's own pace is generally more important than the speed advantage gained by subordinating oneself to group riding.

Randonneurs as Both Bricoleurs and Entrepreneurs
How the distance is covered en route is decided by the randonneur alone. All actions taken are principally the responsibility of the rider. And as long as the rider does not exceed the maximum time limit, the decision as to how a distance is travelled remains with the rider. Routes and checkpoints are devised so as to ensure that the minimum distance requirements will be met even if riders deviate from suggested routes. The tacit knowledge and understanding necessary for long-distance riding are gained through riding itself. Again, this takes time and practice. The skills acquired in the course of one's riding career are put to the test during the brevets. The capacity of the riders is measured less in terms of

their physical superiority than their ability to carefully handle sleep deficits, psychological barriers, inclement weather such as cold and wet conditions, signs of fatigue and the simultaneous struggle to overcome hundreds or even thousands of metres of climbing.

Long-distance cycling requires adaptability. No matter whether one identifies oneself as a *bricoleur* (Levi-Strauss, 1966) assembling and collaging possibilities of action from the many possibilities encountered, or as an *entrepreneur* (Duymedjian & Ansart, 2007) self-reliantly inventive, the capacity to detect and develop one's own creative skills is always important. Reliable action comes before short-term experimentation. Only the experienced randonneur knows how to successfully pass the testing of the self – whether as a capably handy bricoleur or with disciplined entrepreneurship, benefitting from reliable empirical knowledge for innovative solutions and thus using (time) options to the rider's benefit. Both these approaches to skill contrast with the focused expertise and finely honed skill required of, and developed by, the successful sporting rider, whose development can be concentrated on the specific event-oriented training and discipline of the body. Improvisation here is about reading the unfolding patterns of others taking part, rather than reacting to externalities of the ride.

The Randonneur Bike as an Artefact of Progress?

Long-distance cyclists use a specialized but original and traditional artefact, traceable to the age of industrialization. Their styles of bicycle are not obviously competitive machines. Yet the bicycle accelerated social and technical development like no other industrial artefact (Radkau, 2008) – a development that takes into account the human body (Ebert, 2006). The bicycle is a modern tool for accelerating social change (Rosa, 2005, p. 125; Hobsbawm, 2006, p. 112) that has achieved gendered freedom (Bleckmann, 1998; Maierhof & Schröder 1992), also both Cox and van der Kloof this volume). Although technical development of cycles has been subject to numerous highly differentiated refinements (Burrows, 2001), the drivetrain system, frame design and riding position of most racing bicycles has not undergone essential change for more than 100 years (Pooch, 2009). Indeed, the regulations governing the racing bicycle ensure that degrees of innovation are relatively modest. Even when cycle design exhibits radical changes in riding position, the machine – be it a "classical" racing bicycle, a recumbent bicycle or a Velomobile – does not allow for different physical motions due to its technical design (Ückert, 2004; Gressmann, 1995). The body is constrained to the regulation of movement by the processes of pedalling and steering.

In contrast to the minimalist racing cycle, the classic randonneur bicycle has specific features resulting from the specific requirements of the events, for example, cycling at night. Most randonneur machines will be equipped with an efficient and powerful hub dynamo to generate power for bright lights. Notably, prior to the widespread commercial availability of efficient high power LED cycling lights, randonneurs pioneered and shared their own home-made lighting systems to provide sufficient light with minimum power consumption. The randonneur tends to fall back on reliable and ever-functioning light sources instead of using battery-powered lights with a lifetime measured in hours, even though driving the dynamo consumes additional physical power.

Excessively lightweight design of the machine and components, though saving weight (and therefore the work required) risks breakage. Lightweight tyres, though faster running, run greater risk of puncture. The long-distance machine must be designed as an extremely reliable partner in a systemic view of long-distance cycling. Seeking ever lighter material and using thin tyres is common practice among those pursuing maximum speed. The long-distance cyclist accepts the additional burden of greater weight for additional reliability, and the rolling resistance penalties of more puncture-resistant tyres.

The familiar layout of the classic safety bike, however, does not allow for any further significant aerodynamic advancement. Time trial machines with their deep tuck are highly unsuited to the requirements of long duration and self-reliance: comfort (and often manoeuvrability) sacrificed for maximum speed gain. In terms of the acceleration of design, recumbent bicycles and Velomobiles promise speed increases thanks to their aerodynamic design (Pooch, 2009). Not governed by the regulations of international cycle sport, the randonneur is free to choose any design of machine, unrestricted by the rules which banned recumbent bicycles from conventional cycle sport in 1934. Consequently, the number of unconventional designs has increased in the past years both in training and events and they are now a regular feature of Paris-Brest-Paris and other distance rides where allowed (van Donselaar, 2011). The increasing use of recumbent bicycles and Velomobiles shows that these cycles have meanwhile reached a degree of reliability that is equivalent to that of the classic randonneur bikes. Moreover, they also reduce the risk of injury of exposed parts of the body and offer higher degrees of comfort.

Randonneurs and Change
Amateur cycle sport offers not only programmed experiences (in the form of events) but also rapid stringing together of contingencies, requiring improvisational responses. Some participants accept even negative experiences that guarantee venturing into illegality by drug-taking (Hettfleisch, 2009) in order to get the ultimate kick out of steadily riding at 40 km/h (or 25 mph) in open events. Short-distance, high speed events require the mastery of certain body techniques, for example eating and drinking on the bike, rapidly sprinting to regain the safety of the peloton (which causes extremely high heart rates),

even peeing while on the move into a bottle (for men). All have to be part of the training routine to become practised habits.

In comparison with this, the acceleration of technical and social change (Rosa, 2005) in randonneuring seems to be less obvious. Randonneurs are spared the rapid variance of cycling rhythms on the physical side and they rely on tried-and-tested methods on the technical side, eschewing fashionable and lightweight, high-tech components. Similarly, additional body techniques for training or conditioning (Kay & Laberge, 2004) that go beyond the familiar tend to be avoided.

From a physical perspective, undertaking a steady, uniform and repetitive body movement for hours on end, promises neither excitement nor change. This machine-like activity is pursued for hours and days and must not be put at risk carelessly for the sake of hunger for short-term gain or adventure. Mentally, these long hours of repetition are also a significant challenge. Long distances give the cyclist a chance to sink into a slowed-down way of life. The comparatively slower speed may be regarded as "conservative" practice in a world of organized leisure cycling that is otherwise based on values like speed and action. The older average age of randonneurs confronts the image of cycling as an activity for young and athletic types: a significant proportion of randonneurs are of retirement age. It challenges the high performance world of a sport struggling with the legacy and image of doping. It also challenges the onlooker to reconsider the capability of older participants.

In this sense, randonneurs should be regarded as preservers of continuity rather than agents of change. Yet when we examine some of the trends in current randonneuring, such as the use of specialist cycles to optimize speed, we can see a contrary tendency. Other innovations, such as the physical optimization of sleep by power napping (Rosa, 2005), or the transfer of group riding techniques from road racing are

certainly discussed by riders (http://www.heinemann-pbp. de
/idee.html).

These technologies and techniques, however, become less
efficacious as distances increase. The further the distance, the
more important is the specific practice and condition of any
individual rider and machine. The long distance ride is
absolutely dominated by the rider's own rhythm of cycling and
the associated knowledge of the body. To find others with
exactly the same pace is unlikely. In this context, achieving
higher speeds in a group has its limitations. Riding (faster) in a
group over long distances would logically bring the stronger
riders to the front and leave others behind to follow if possible.
Then the test no longer becomes one of the self.

To achieve this, randonneurs would have to submit
themselves to the group and become disciplined subordinates.
The experiences of those who have tried this method confirm
that the overall outcomes of such practices are not positive:
"racing as a team over this long distance turned out to be rather
obstructive even when it provided a better time to our fittest
riders" (http://www.heinemann-pbp.de/news.html). This is
despite the shared knowledge that cycling alone is less rapid
and more work. Where riding with others becomes important
for the randonneur is in the maintenance of mental, rather than
physical strength. Riding side by side for company rather than
in tandem for shelter is a more common sight on a brevet.

Conclusions
There is little change in the percentage of riders who complete
Paris-Brest-Paris, demonstrating that the entrepreneur-brico-
leur-DIY approach is an appropriate tactic for the work-
hardened, enduring body. The craving for speed exhibited by
some is untypical. The overwhelming number of participants
employ traditional approaches and traditional machines. Breaks
with tradition are slower than with other groups of amateur
riders. Novice sporting riders sometimes act as if sophisticated

bikes can replace training and exercise. Every randonneur knows by experience that riding long distances takes more than just pedalling and an extreme aero posture. But this knowledge take time to accumulate. Experience is a privilege of age and of the availability of hours to spend on the bike. The world of randonneuring can appear from the outside as difficult to enter and relatively exclusive. For this reason, in the UK, for example, shorter distance (60–100 km) randonnées are often run parallel to longer ones to provide a means of access into what otherwise would remain (in appearance) a closed world.

The value system in randonneuring has been relatively stable to date. This partly stems from the fact that riders are not participating in professionally organized, media-promoted sports events. Consequently, doping makes little sense. On the contrary, the achievement of a brevet rests on the ability to build lasting relationships between rider and machine. The arrival of the "many" and not the success of a "few" – brought about by the "drudgery" of many – is what counts in the end of the ride. Organized co-operatively and by volunteers, randonneuring is self-governed. This contrasts with the business of leisure-sport and professional sport, both of which ultimately rely on the exploitation of the individual and where winners are defined as those who are most competitive and opportunistic against other participants.

Is this to argue that randonneurs can be the future saviours of cycling, or even cycle sport? Certainly not. The extent of the necessary body-work is beyond the general comprehension of a society almost exclusively oriented to short-duration physical activity. The brevet distances seem supernatural and hardly conceivable to an outsider. Access to these levels of endurance seems almost as difficult as access to the levels of (speed-oriented) fitness required to participate at high levels of cycle sport. Neither activity connects in any meaningful sense with the everyday riding discussed in other chapters in this volume.

The structure of other types of organized road riding is also changing. Sportive events put less stress on fast finishing times, and more emphasis on personal achievement. There are also signs that the world of brevet riding and the (non-competitive) sportive riding are coming much closer together. There are examples of multi-day sportives (for example London–Edinburgh in two or four days), in which a strong spirit of co-operation between participants can be observed. These longer rides insist on a degree of self-sufficiency on the road, if only for ease of organization. Commercial organizers needing to ensure participation rates (sales of entry) focus on the experiential dimensions of the whole event, not just the chance to prove oneself as fast as possible. Boundaries are beginning to blur a little. Perhaps the biggest difference is that these are financially costly events to enter, compared with the brevet ride which remains firmly and identifiably self-organized. Other differences remain in relation to how far event organizers seek to mimic the styles and practices of professional cycle sport, for example by restricting the type of cycle to be ridden: some sportives ban recumbents and Velomobiles, others welcome them.

Organized leisure cycling today offers the participant perhaps more choices than ever before. From traditional cycling clubs, various forms of racing, sportive events and brevet rides can all be found in a variety of locations, with different stresses found in different events. While all may look like and fit a category of organized leisure, closer examination shows that we can discern some very different bodily practices and requirements across a range of disciplines and types of event. In examining randonneuring we see tensions between images of innovation and conservatism, between the freedom to define one's own progress and the intense discipline of the body and will to sufficiently cope with the demands of endurance. We have also seen how different the demands of these practices are from other forms of riding.

Randonneuring provides an example of a very specific subculture of activity. A world of riding with its own rules and expectations, viewed from outside even by some sportive cyclists interviewed as extreme and unusual. Yet within its own circles operate supportive, open networks, ready to support and share with fellow participants. There is a strong sense of competitiveness, of the desire to overcome, but it is focused on one's own limits, not on the overcoming of others. If we are looking for wider implications, then perhaps it is this refocusing and redefinition of the meaning and practices of competition that is significant. What would be the impact if professional cyclists in the Tour de France, as role models for leisure cycle-sport, would have to repair their machines on their own? What if they had to become self-sufficient instead of relying on the division of labour (Teuffel, 2012)?

Acknowledgements

An early version of this chapter was previously published as H. Bunte (2012). Randonneurship – eine moderne radsportinszenierung. *Sozialwissenschaften und Berufspraxis*, 35(1), 60–69.

References

Bette, K.-H. (2004). *X-treme: Zur Soziologie des Abenteuer- und Risikosports*. Bielefeld, Germany: Transcript-Verlag.

Bleckmann, D. (1998). *Wehe wenn sie losgelassen! Über die Anfänge des Frauenradfahrens in Deutschland*. Gera-Leipzig, Germany: Maxime, Verlag Maxi Kutschera.

Bunte, H. (2009). *Randonneurship – eine Individualisierte, Außerbetriebliche Form des Erwerbs von Metaqualifikationen?* Unpublished Master's Thesis, Hamburg, Germany.

Burrows, M. (2001). *Bicycle Design: Towards the Perfect Machine*. London, UK: Company of Cyclist Publications.

Déon, B. (1997). *Une légende centenaire: Paris-Brest et retour.* Raviéres, France: B. Déon.

Die Drogenbeauftragte der Bundesregierung, (2011). Drogen- und Suchtbericht 2011. http://drogenbeauftragte.de/ fileadmin/dateien/Publikationen/Drogen_Sucht/Forschu ngsberichte/Bericht_Drogen-_und_Suchtbericht_2011.pdf [last modified 26 June 2013].

Duymedjian, R., & Ansart, S. (2007). From the Creative Destructor to the Entrepreneur-Bricoleur. A Contribution to Schumpeter's Theory of Entrepreneurial Innovation. In E.G. Carayannis & C. Ziemnowicz (eds.), *Rediscovering Schumpeter* (pp. 143–170). Basingstoke, UK: Palgrave Macmillan.

Ebert, A.-K. (2006). Zwischen "Radreiten" und "Kraftmaschine". Der bürgerliche Radsport am Ende des 19. Jahrhunderts. *WerkstattGeschichte Sport*, 15(44), 27–45.

Eckstein, H. (2011). http://www.droplimits.de/index.php/ paris-brest-paris-201/articles/fahrerbericht-von-hajo-eckstein. html) [last modified 26 June 2013].

Friel, J. (2007). *Die Trainingsbibel für Radsportler.* Bielefeld, Germany: Covadonga.

Gressmann, M. (1995). *Fahrradphysik und Biomechanik: Technik, Formeln, Gesetze.* [sixth edition]. Kiel, Germany: Moby-Dick-Verlag.

Hettfleisch, W. (2009). Giro d'Italia: Alte Sünder im rosaroten Taumel. Der Jubiläums Giro blendet das Doping aus. *Frankfurter Rundschau* 16 May 2009. http://www.fr-online.de/sport/92--giro-d-italia-alte-suender-im-rosaroten-taumel,1472784,3362742.html [last modified 23 June 2013].

Hobsbawm, E. (2006). *Gefährliche Zeiten: Ein Leben im 20. Jahrhundert.* München, Germany: Deutscher Taschenbuch Verlag. [Previously published (2003) as *Interesting Times: A Twentieth-Century Life.* London, UK: Pantheon.]

Kay, J., & Laberge, S. (2004). Mandatory Equipment. Women in Adventure Racing. In B. Wheaton (ed.), *Understanding Lifestyle Sports: Consumption, Identity and Difference* (pp. 154–174). London, UK: Routledge.

Leibbrand, O. (2008). Zur Geschichte des bürgerlichen Radsports im Deutschen Kaiserreich. *SportZeiten. Sport in Geschichte, Kultur und Gesellschaft, 8*(3), 79–105.

Levi-Strauss, C. (1966). *The Savage Mind.* Chicago, IL: University of Chicago Press.

Lindner, W. (2005). *Radsporttraining: Methodische Erkenntnisse, Trainingsgestaltung, Leistungsdiagnostik* [fifth edition]. München, Germany: Blv Verlag.

Lüders, O. (1925). *Der Radfahrsport: Wandern, Turnen, Spiel und Sport zu Rade.* Berlin, Germany: Ullstein.

Maierhof, G., & Schröder, K. (1992). *Sie radeln wie ein Mann, Madame: Wie die Frauen das Rad eroberten.* Zürich, Switzerland: Unionsverl.

Moll, S. (2000). Droge Sport. *Tour – Das Radmagazin, 9,* 46–51.

Neumann, G., Pfützner, A., & Berbalk, A. (1999). *Optimiertes Ausdauertraining.* Aachen, Germany: Meyer & Meyer Fachverlag.

Oddy, N. (2007). The Flaneur on Wheels. In D. Horton, P. Rosen, & P. Cox (eds.), *Cycling and Society* (pp. 97–112). Aldershot, UK: Ashgate Publishing.

Pooch, A. (2009). *Die Wissenschaft vom schnellen Radfahren* (second edition). Troisdorf, Germany: Liegerad-Datei-Verlag.

Radkau, J. (2008). *Technik in Deutschland: Vom 18. Jahrhundert bis heute.* Frankfurt, Germany: Campus Verlag.

Rosa, H. (2005). *Beschleunigung: Die Veränderung der Zeitstrukturen in der Moderne.* Frankfurt am Main, Germany: Suhrkamp.

Schenkel, E. (2008). *Cyclomanie: Fahrrad und Literatur.* Eggingen, Germany: Edition Isele.

Schröder, R. (2000). *Paris-Brest-Paris. 1200 Kilometer nonstop: Eine persönliche Erinnerung an ein außergewöhnliches Rennen.* Nordersted, Germany: Books on Demand.

Shilling, C. (2003). *The Body and Social Theory* (second edition). London, UK: SAGE Publications.

Teuffel, F. (2012). Der Sport hat jede Vorbildwirkung verloren. Interview mit dem Philosophen Gunter Gebauer. *Der Tagesspiegel*, 8 January 2012. http://www.tagesspiegel.de/sport/interview-mit-philosoph-gebauer-der-sport-hat-jede-vorbildwirkung-verloren/6043076.html [last modified 26 June 2013].

Ückert, S. (2004). *Kinematische und dynamische Aspekte der Binnenstruktur von Tretkurbelbewegungen: Bewegungstheoretische und trainingswissenschaftliche Bedingungen in Abhängigkeit von Widerstand und Frequenz.* Aachen, Germany: Shaker.

van Donselaar, G. (2011). Mens en machine in Paris-Brest-Paris. *Ligfiets&*, 27 (6), 35–37.

Voss, G. (1991). *Lebensfuhrung als Arbeit: Über die Autonomie der Person im Alltag der Gesellschaft.* Stuttgart, Germany: F. Enke.

CHAPTER 8

WOMEN, GENDERED ROLES, DOMESTICITY AND CYCLING IN BRITAIN, 1930-1980

Peter Cox

Introduction: The Gendered Bicycle

The safety bicycle is a quintessentially gendered object (Oddy, 1995). The existence of two distinct styles – diamond and open frame – is not based on human biological difference but on the expectations of the type of clothing to be worn by the rider. The diamond frame requires the rider to wear divided leg garments, the step-through, open frame being designed to allow the rider to wear full skirts. Although step-through frames have a whole range of advantages in ease of use, such is the ubiquity of this gendering of the artefact that the terms ladies' and gents' bicycles are still expected today when bicycles are described. As an aside, it is perhaps worth observing that my last insurance policy could not cope with the possibility that the bicycle was neither a "gent's" nor "ladies'" model. Faulkner (2001) points out that such gendered technologies also both conform to, and reproduce, broader normative roles. In the case of the bicycle, a discourse of normalcy arises, such that the diamond frame is not just the default design, but "normal" or "proper": variations on it become "other" and of lesser value (see Salleh, 1997 for a broader philosophical treatment of this theme). It was not until the advent of the small-wheeled, "F-Frame" Moulton bicycle in the UK at the end of 1962 that there was a mass-produced bicycle designed and marketed explicitly for "universal" or "unisex" use. Frequently, however, it was derided in reviews as not being a "proper", or "man's" bicycle precisely for its lack of a top tube. (Which begs the question of whether the top tube acts as a penis substitute.)

Women and Cycling in Britain

Discussions of the early relationship of women and the bicycle are relatively well rehearsed, especially in relation to the "new woman" (Bleckmann, 1998; McGurn, 1999; Norcliffe, 2001; Strange & Brown, 2002; Herlihy, 2004; and Ebert, 2010). Although arguments circulated about the inappropriateness of bicycles for women in the late nineteenth century, these were curtly dismissed in most quarters: "A woman no more sits upon her genital organs when riding the bicycle than a man sits upon his when riding a horse" ("Cycling for Women", 1894). Women's ridership during the years after the First World War, as the bicycle became mass transport in the UK, is less well examined. This chapter approaches the relationship of women, gendered roles and the bicycle with a specific focus on the United Kingdom, and largely through cyclo-tourism, that is, cycling conducted for its own sake, as an explicit leisure pursuit. Much of the activity of cycle tourism was conducted through the aegis of organized cycle clubs. Indeed the Cyclists' Touring Club (CTC) in the UK was the very first bicycle club, founded in 1878: well before the advent of the safety bicycle. The period under study here is, roughly speaking therefore, the second fifty years of the CTC.

At its half centenary in 1928, the club was dealing with a number of simultaneous problems. Rapidly increasing numbers of bicycles on the road, mainly for utility use; increasing accident rates, especially due to conflict with the growing numbers of motorists; and tensions between the club's traditional middle-class touring membership and the need for it to act as a representative body for all cyclists in the face of largely hostile social elites, all required consideration. It was in this context that the CTC began to address the issue of women and cycling as a specific topic.

The monthly *CTC Gazette*, together with its successor *Cycletouring* (from 1963), provides a snapshot insight into the expressed concerns of organized UK leisure cyclists through the twentieth century. While not necessarily or definitively representative, we can use archival material to provide an insight into the ways in which processes of identity are constructed and social norms are advanced (compare Johnson & Lloyd, 2004; Deegan this volume). The half-century span considered allows comparison of the construction of women's roles across a rapidly changing social landscape. We should also be reminded that this span can be framed in a single lifetime. In the October/November 1977 issue of *Cycletouring*, a two-page illustrated article featured an interview with 90-year-old Ivy Donaldson, still riding almost a half century after taking part in her first overseas CTC tour in 1929. This and other biographical examples may assist in conceptualizing how we understand macro-level changes in both practices and discursive processes and relate them back from the sociological abstract to the personal and experiential.

Women and Cycling at the End of the 1920s

By the end of the 1920s, cycling was a normal means of transport for a substantial proportion of workers. It also remained an archetypal leisure pursuit for the lower middle classes in Britain. Notably, Langhamer (2000) makes the observation that cycling was a cheaper leisure pursuit than others, since, once a bicycle had been acquired, little other financial outlay was required, unlike the trip costs incurred in, for example, rambling, and no further transport costs accrued. But it was still the lower-middle-class riders who formed the majority of the CTC membership. The total number of cyclists in 1930 was estimated in Parliament to be around 7,000,000 (Nathan, 1930). There is some difficulty in obtaining accurate figures for this period, but French bicycle registration was over 7 million at the end of the 1920s and was understood at the time to be similar to, or slightly less than, the UK. Compared with this mass bicycle usage, the 28,000 CTC membership was numerically insignificant, but the organization was at the forefront of defining a representative role against widespread social prejudice against cyclists (Cox, 2012).

The *Gazette* was the mouthpiece of the organization for CTC members, sharing news of events and activities, developments in the trade, and classified advertisements. The bulk of each issue's copy comprised reports on touring: describing rides and acting as inspiration and aspiration for activity. The lively letters page provided a mouthpiece for CTC members themselves to pursue specific topics and to take issue with staff writers. The very celebration of touring and leisure activities – against a national background of mass unemployment and the level of social inequalities that led to the hunger marches – indicates how firmly rooted in middle-class experience and lifestyle the CTC was at this point (Gardiner, 2010). In relation to expanding cyclist numbers in the 1930s, the *Gazette* grew in confidence both as a news sharing service, gathering reports and comments on cyclists in press and parliament, and ultimately developing an advocacy role in response to perceived threats.

If the tone of the *Gazette* was firmly lower-middle-class, then it should also be noted that it was precisely lower-middle-class women who were seeing the most dramatic transformations in lifestyle in the interwar years. Marriage remained the socially expected norm, despite the perceived shortage of eligible men. Nationally, some 5.5 to 6 million women were in work, but 84% of these were single, widowed or divorced. Marriage, especially for middle-class women, generally signalled a retreat into the confines of the domestic sphere. Once married, a woman was expected to re-orient her primary concerns around home and household. It was to these women that a new genre of women's magazines, for example *Woman's Own* founded in 1932, was addressed. Yet the sharp division between single and married lifestyle patterns was not unchallenged and it was this particular divide that was strongly addressed in the pages of the *Gazette*.

The articulation of a specific stance vis-à-vis the modern woman cyclotourist was forcefully made in May 1930, in an article headed "Cycling in Childhood". A guest writer under the pseudonym of "Petronella" wrote, "Motherhood is the greatest thing in Life, but there is no reason why every other joy in life should be given up for it" (*Gazette*, May, p. 170). She suggested that there was no need to spend more than six months off the bike around the birth of a child. Once a child was three months old, she argued, a "well-sprung sidecar" attached to a tandem could provide an eminently suitable baby carriage, with the added advantage that it made the carrying of camping gear easier.

"Petronella" was a CTC Councillor, Mrs E. Parkes, vice-president of Shropshire District Association (DA) and the wife of a Midlands cycle manufacturer. The CTC was, and still is, organized at local level through DAs, local clubs autonomously responsible for organizing rides and other social events. It was run by a series of elected councillors at various levels. She was therefore, relatively well placed within the organization and not a marginal figure. Her links to manufacturing should not be taken to indicate a connection to large-scale production, however. Throughout the period under consideration, alongside large-scale manufacturer for the mass market, craft-scale or independent artisanal building of bespoke frames was relatively common in the touring scene.

Although outwardly reinforcing the social role of women as mothers, Petronella's advice can also be read as undermining existing expectations of appropriate behaviour in motherhood. The tenor of the article illustrates a tension which was to recur in the *Gazette* for the next decade. The destiny of women in marriage, and in taking responsibility for childrearing and domestic life, was not in itself challenged. But in contrast to the observance of these wider social mores, cycling, properly organized, was being presented as a means by which the restriction of these activities within the domestic household could be broken. Where motherhood conventionally signalled withdrawal from public life (and into dependence) for the middle-class woman, Petronella's advice was a direct confrontation. The gendered division of labour remained unchallenged, but the public/private spatial segregation assumed to be integral to it is redefined. Debates on the appropriate social and domestic roles were certainly not unique to the CTC, but part of a broader response to dramatic changes in fertility rates in post-First World War marriage and the consequent renegotiation of familial roles (Irwin, 2003). The social roles of single women were changing, especially as a significant number of older women remained single. Echoes can also be heard here of previous generations of explicitly *socialist* cycling advocacy: that the bicycle could provide the means by which the countryside and public space could be made available to all, not just remaining the preserve of a privileged few (Pye, 1995; Cox, 2015).

Similarly, Petronella's advice can be seen to reflect earlier framing of the relation of the bicycle to women's emancipation. While living in London in 1927, the American socialist feminist, Crystal Eastman, reflected that "Bicycles were the beginning of women's emancipation" (Eastman, 1978). What they had offered to the previous generation was the opportunity for unchaperoned, autonomous and independent mobility: precisely those codes of action constrained by rigid social roles. Eastman and other militant feminists campaigned through the 1920s for the abolition of laws and provisions for the special protection of women, arguing that equality for women must mean equality at all levels (see especially her writings in *Time and Tide*). Whilst not explicitly advocating women's equality, Petronella's initial column can be read as an implicit endorsement of what were, at the time, radical feminist views.

The small-scale and artisanal production, alongside a creative "do-it yourself" mentality fostered in the club, provided the technologies that made this liberation possible. Tandems were much more common in the UK in the 1930s than in the early twenty-first century, and (apparently) used in greater numbers in the UK than elsewhere in continental Europe. The reason for their greater availability may well lie in the relative proliferation of independent manufacture. Individual cycle businesses would often braze their own frames from standardized tube and lug-sets. Thus tailor-made bicycles and short batch, individualized production were more common than they are today and tandems, especially, benefit from bespoke construction to match the riders' physiques. Frequently ridden by mixed couples on social rides, tandems became a means publicly to signal the connection between the riders. Numbers were sufficient for some CTC DAs to organize specific tandem and family "runs" (as rides are generally known). "Juvenile Sidecars" were built and advertised by numerous recognized manufacturers, but were also frequently home-fabricated by enthusiastic riders. Family cycling became a regular feature of photographic reporting in the *Gazette*. The sidecar functioned as an enabling device for both parents of children, allowing them to continue with normal social life.

If the first barrier to be overcome concerned *when* women could and should ride, a second obvious question concerned *how far*? A letter published in the *Gazette's* correspondence pages later that same year, posed exactly that question: "How far should Ladies ride?". The author tentatively suggested that, "my own idea has been that providing no ill effects are felt there can be little harm in going as far as you wish, and this distance for me, averages about 70 miles" (August 1930, p. 287). The *Gazette* firmly responded that:

> lady members of the club commonly ride much greater distances than those mentioned, and there can be no possible

harm if there is no feeling of exhaustion. Naturally some women can cover many more miles in a day than others, even 300 having been exceeded by one of our lady officials.

A third question, concerning *where* to ride, can be illustrated through the recollections of Ivy Donaldson, (mentioned above). She was one of four women riders (out of nineteen) who took part in a CTC guided tour in the Alps during the summer of 1929. Donaldson was given no more than a short interview at CTC head office to assess her suitability before embarking. Three weeks later the group had ridden no fewer than fourteen Alpine passes, including the 9,000 ft Stelvio. Many of these routes were still unsurfaced at this time. The answer to the question of where to ride appeared to be "anywhere you want". Note also, that here we have single women participating in a mixed group holiday. In the wake of enfranchisement and of rapid changes in employment law and practices, it appears that the idea of appropriate and inappropriate leisure behaviours for women was also in a state of flux.

"Wheelwisdom for Women"

In the *Gazette* of September 1930, (p. 321), hope was expressed "to make the 'ladies' page a regular feature", and from the following month it became so: a one- or two-page feature, appearing under the headline of "Wheelwisdom for Women", written by "Petronella". One may speculate on the choice of pen name. Ford Madox Ford's poem "To Petronella at Sea" had not long been published (there shall be no refuge for you and me/ who haste away) but another, perhaps more likely, reference might be to the powerful and influential twelfth-century Countess of Leicester, recorded in chronicles as a woman in her own right, not just as wife of Earl Robert (Johns, 2003). The column, usually a page, sometimes two, was to run for a decade until the summer of 1940, when the *Gazette* reduced in volume as restrictions on paper were imposed. The topics of these monthly articles are remarkable inasmuch as the concerns reflected in them have become perennial topics for discussion of women and cycling, in successive generations of cycling magazines, and now, today, in online forums.

The September 1931 article focuses on correct adjustments to clothing and cycles for fellow riders. "I have wondered how many girls there are who have given up the game, feeling that they are physically unsuited for it, when it is, perhaps, only their machines and equipment that are unsuitable." (p. 321). Further, it recommended that the solution to these basic problems was in some degree of familiarity with machine: "It has been said that women have unmechanical minds. This is, I believe, like most generalities, untrue. It is not women's minds that are at fault but their training." (p. 321). The reason for frequent inappropriate choices and for lack of mechanical aptitude was also identified.

> That is the worst part of being a woman; there are so many jobs that our menfolk consider are not fitted for us, and they have carried us about for so long that it is small wonder if we have become, for the most part, just bundles of inhibitions.

Petronella's advice was gently revolutionary.

The initial (September 1930) foray into the subject of children and cycling prompted a number of letters in response. To appease those who expressed dislike of the effects of sidecars on handling, a photograph in the October issue (p. 373) showed a home-built design of child-seat. Maintaining a tone gently subversive of roles, this was shown on a cycle ridden by a male rider, whilst immediately adjacent was another picture showing the award of the Dunlop challenge cup for a women's race at Herne Hill velodrome, as if to offset the exclusive association of women's cycling with childcare and domestic concern. The third news item in the column was the announcement of an initial set of classes to be given by a professional mechanic in Birmingham to offset the general lack of mechanical training provided to women in normal social and educational activity. Other training schemes run by members around the country involved in the trade, continued to be mentioned throughout the following decade. Even in the twenty-first century, this topic is still perceived as a particular problem, tackled by, for example, the *Wenches with Wrenches* programme (see Welke & Allen, 2004).

Allied to the issue of the mechanical aptitude (or not) of women, the question of appropriate bicycle design was also a frequent topic of discussion. Bicycles designed and marketed for women have, since the 1890s, been characterized by a lack of a top tube (running horizontally from just below handlebars to just below saddle), a style usually described as "open frame". Note the definition of women's frames as "lacking" a top tube, even the language assisting the gendering patterns. The usual substitution of this top tube with a parallel down tube (from above the steering forks to the crank axle) tends to make the frame more flexible. This characteristic is exacerbated when the bicycle is laden for touring: hence the reason why "women's" frames were frequently criticized. (Modern open frames avoid this problem by using use large diameter hydroformed aluminium tubing.) The advent of a dropped top tube frame – where the top tube meets the seat tube halfway up – was seen by Petronella to be an encouraging innovation at the 1930 Olympia Cycle Show (*Gazette*, December 1930, p. 432). The second problem with cycles marketed for women was that they were almost always significantly heavier than their diamond framed counterparts (18–20 lbs for a standard lightweight, 25 lbs for a women's model).

For touring and other leisure use, Petronella argued continually that women should ride the best cycles possible, ideally a standard diamond frame. Only the continued wearing of skirts whilst riding could necessitate a deviation from this. However, it was also recognized that those women who used cycles for everyday purposes, for work rather than leisure, still needed to wear skirts and so clear distinction had to be made between machines for everyday and leisure cycling. "When will they [manufacturers] wake up to the fact that there is a big and ever-growing demand for a really light, speedy, well built and good-looking open framed machine?" she asked (*Gazette*, November 1932, p. 342). Instead, working women were forced to ride heavy utility machines even when their tasks necessitated considerable amounts of riding.

We should not assume that utility riding during this period was somewhat incidental and only of low mileage. An example provided in the *Gazette* (May 1939, p. 147) was of two city nurses who, in the first three months of 1939, accumulated totals of 900 and 780 miles respectively, fully laden with all their bags and equipment. Given that "women's cycles" constituted 22–25% of the output of a major manufacturer such as BSA, and that significant numbers of women rode standard diamond frame cycles, the potential market was not an inconsiderable one (*Gazette*, December 1939, p. 339). By mid 1940 the proportion had doubled to 48%. (*Gazette*, July 1940, p. 155). The failure of manufacturers to recognize this market-share was vocally lamented.

The "lightweight" was a peculiarly British machine – a sporting bicycle (with "dropped" handlebars to accommodate multiple hand positions for long rides) but equipped with mudguards and saddlebag. It was constantly reaffirmed as essential to the idea of riding for pleasure (*Gazette*, November 1930, p. 402). Although utility might be got from a town bike, only the agility and easy running of a lightweight, it was considered, could allow the rider, male or female, to truly take pleasure in riding. Reports of tours in Germany, Denmark and the Netherlands frequently commented on the rarity of British-style lightweights and suggested a direct correlation of the relative scarcity of touring and leisure riding in those destinations. In line with the extension of pleasure riding to a greater audience, "Wheelwisdom" also regularly reported on and supported a wider variety of local rides organized by DAs. Of especial note were "Loiterers' Runs". The word has slightly shifted in meaning and connotation since the 1930s, but these were designed to be ridden at a gentler pace, with more opportunity to stop and linger; an easy way to introduce newcomers to social riding in a more convivial atmosphere.

Petronella's interventions into women-specific equipment came in response to experience. "[F]rom my correspondence it is obvious that far too big a percentage of girls suffer from saddle-soreness and in some cases the riding of an unsuitable saddle has led to lasting injury". Consequently many women were being forced to adapt to existing saddles "instead of being able to select a saddle most likely to suit her from a range designed anatomically for women" (*Gazette*, September 1933, p. 295). Women's saddles, designed for a broader pelvis, had been widely advertised and produced from the 1890s. Petronella was identifying a specific sector of the quality leather-saddle market which seems to have disappeared by the end of the 1920s. She was not afraid to be explicitly outspoken on the topic, using her column to respond (without having to print what would clearly have been unpublishable) "Your trouble is caused by pressure on a nerve and I should imagine that your saddle is to blame. Make sure that you are not sitting too high." (*Gazette*, October 1934, p. 357.) This ultimately resulted in the production by Dunlop of a range of women-specific leather touring saddles.

Clothing and Femininity

Of all the topics to vex not only women correspondents but also to provoke male comment was the subject of dress. In Petronella's words, "of all the questions that affect feminine cyclists there is one that always seems to be recurring. It is the question of clothes" (*Gazette*, February 1937, p. 36). Petronella firmly advocated plus fours or shorts, according to the weather, coupled with layered wool and silk to protect against winter cold (see *Gazette*, January 1931, p. 7; March 1932, p. 68; January 1934, p. 31; July 1934, p. 237). Divided skirts, although popular with a number of women, and apparently especially popular in the Netherlands and Austria (*Gazette*, August 1937, p. 269) were not her preferred solution. However she was prepared to accept that they allowed some to feel more comfortable and patterns were even discussed (*Gazette*, August 1934, p. 239).

For some CTC members, shorts remained anathema, even on men. On women, they were truly beyond the pale (see correspondence from CTC Board member C. W. Cooke, *Gazette*, March 1931, p. 90). Although shorts or plus fours provided ideal riding wear, when touring women faced the problem of the unacceptability of shorts once dismounted. Petronella's preferred solution was to carry a wrap-around skirt in the top on the saddlebag which could be put on quickly and without difficulty so as not to cause offence (*Gazette*, July 1934, p. 238). In this, as in all her interventions, Petronella's approach was first and foremost dominated by pragmatism, especially when touring abroad:

> Each country has its own ideas about women's attire (curiously enough, none of them seem to trouble about what the men wear) and my own rule in this matter is put in a nutshell by the proverb "When in Rome do as Rome does" with the mental reservation, 'more or less' (*Gazette*, September 1935, pp. 337–338).

Ultimately, the issue of clothing remained as much an issue of liberty and of rights as it had been in the era of rational dress campaigning. But Petronella did not hold out hope that rationality would hold sway over tradition and prejudice.

> It is about time that girl cyclists were allowed to dress as they like (within reason) and as they consider most suitable for the type of riding they prefer … I say it is *time* that all these things should come to pass. It is – but I have not the slightest hope that they really will, and even if I did have any hope at all I expect that it would be entirely dashed to pieces when I read the replies that I shall surely get to these remarks. (*Gazette*, October 1937, p. 342)

The kind of critic she was thinking about had not been reticent in responding throughout the life of the column. For example, a letter in the March 1932 edition (p. 80) read:

> I regard "Petronella" as a keen enthusiast of the wheel game, but I am not keen to hear too much "more of the ladies". We might shortly hear too much! Cycling is a man's game first and foremost and I would not wish there to be anything effeminate about the *Gazette*.

Nevertheless, such complaints remained a minority and ultimately, "Wheelwisdom for Women" became the most popular feature in the *Gazette* across the whole of its readership (*Gazette*, April 1938, p. 112). In its ten years of publication it ensured that Petronella's depiction and analysis of the proper role of women was far more influential than might initially be thought from a single writer. Yet these perceptions did not appear to spread to manufacturers and advertisers in the *Gazette*: their copy continued to portray largely subordinate and decorative roles for women.

In its discussions of cycle touring, "Wheelwisdom" conforms to expectations of women's primary concern as the domestic. Discussions revolve around the practical minutiae of cycle camping, details of equipment and means to make a tour more successful and more amenable. Suggestions were given for the best way to select and pack bags (*Gazette*, May 1939, p. 147). Instructions were even provided for making one's own ultra-lightweight solo tent (weight about 1 lb) and how in "these days of depression" old camping kit might be shared and basic minimal cost equipment could be made (*Gazette*, June 1933, p. 183). The relative merits and aesthetics of dress styles are a constant theme:

> Why two inches of leg visible above a stocking top [ending below shorts] should look far more disreputable than six inches of bare knee, or even than bare leg and ankle sock, I have not the least idea; I only know that one offends my eye while the other definitely pleases. (*Gazette*, July 1934 p. 237)

Problems of skincare and maintaining a fair complexion are also dealt with (use plenty of vanishing cream and leave it on while riding: *Gazette*, December 1934, p. 421).

Yet, beyond the domesticity and clichéd femininity of these concerns, "Wheelwisdom" was simultaneously advocating solo and independent camping as entirely suitable and appropriate for women. Women, either solo or as paired companions, are regularly depicted, visually as well as in-text (See *Gazette*, June 1939, p. 126). Petronella's own long tour of central Europe in 1937 was in the company of a Mrs Mary Dodds. In subsequent descriptions of their travels, comparison of women's uses of bicycles in various countries provided an ongoing theme. Even the etiquette of shared responsibility in tandeming came under comment. For mixed couples riding tandem she suggested (rather radically and against the general mechanical advice which puts the heavier rider at the front) that they should be free to sort out their own dynamic. It is often more appropriate, she argues, for women to ride as pilot rather than stoker (in the front seat rather than behind) (*Gazette*, November 1935, p. 391). Importantly, this latter is justified by women's social condition: "women as a whole are more highly strung and nervous (I do not mean neurotic), and that the complete faith and self-surrender which a man takes for granted is much more difficult of an attainment than he imagines". Her attribution of these qualities is far from essentialist. She clearly recognizes that these conditions are socially constructed, resulting from women's historic lack of opportunity (see previous comment on mechanical aptitude).

Petronella used comparison with the place and status of women cycling in other European nations to highlight the degree of construction present in gender roles. Reflecting on a tour of Germany in 1936 she commented that current German conceptions of womanhood and manhood ... [are] allied to the fundamental idea of the nation's welfare. ... That has led to the transformation of recreation into training, and – rightly or wrongly – to the condemnation of everything that does not accord with current ideas of womanliness. (October 1936, p. 335)

Implicit recognition was given here to National Socialism's fetishization of women as mothers, and the denigration of activities that might be construed as a "search for pleasure" (Durham, 1998, p. 19). Although appearing to be even-handed and non-political in her writing, the tone is highly critical and she is clearly aggrieved at the social restrictions imposed by pro-natalist discourses and policies (also in place in France at this time). Consistent in her analysis that problems for women were inextricably intertwined with (and constructed through) broader social role expectations, in the early 1930s she had toured in Spain and in the Pyrenees and commented negatively on the likelihood of full emancipation for Spanish women (*Gazette*, November 1931, p. 351). She acknowledged the many changes ("good and bad") brought about by the coming of the republic, but even though the right to vote had been granted she thought that it would need considerable intervention and education for women to take full advantage of its possibilities (*Gazette*, April 1933, p. 115).

The overt concerns of "Wheelwisdom for Women" are domestic detail, the roles and responsibilities of a gender stereotype. More subtly, though, the column acted to redefine women's roles. She acted to change the perception of women as cyclists. Her championing of women as cycle tourists showed them riding for riding's sake and not for ulterior motives, that is, solely for utilitarian need (*Gazette*, January 1939). This may seem insignificant but it carefully places women cycle tourists as social agents. For example, in May 1935 (p. 174) she wrote:

My own impression is that, because the modern girl is trusted more, is not watched so closely and is left more to follow her

189

own devices than to have her actions decided for her, she develops her individuality to a much greater extent, and is not so likely to have an inferiority complex, as was the girl of previous generations.

Alongside championing women as cycle tourists (including "ladies'" [women-only] rides), Petronella also reported in the exploits of women riding in speed and endurance events.

In the 1930s, the dominant form of cycle sport in Britain was the time trial. Massed start road racing was still forbidden by the NCU (National Cyclists' Union). Since 1888, the Roads Records Association (RRA) had ratified claims upon achievements ridden on the road. It recognized rides made by men over given distances (from 25 to 1,000 miles) and times for fixed point-to-point routes. The Women's Road Record Association (WRRA) was founded in the latter half of 1934 to recognize women's achievements and immediately prompted numerous notable rides. By 1939, Petronella could point to a pantheon of (professional) riders who had set significant achievements, which could not only inspire but disprove any idea of women's inherent inferiority (*Gazette*, February 1939, p. 39). Even today, the achievements of these women challenge preconceptions. "Billie" Dovey rode almost 30,000 miles in 1938, touring the country and giving lectures on health and fitness in the evenings. Lilian Dredge set a women's Land's End to John O'Groats (LEJOG) record of 3 days 20 hours and 54 minutes. Pearl Wellington of the Vegetarian Cycling Club broke five WRRA records between 1935 and 1938. Marguerite Wilson set records at distances from 10 miles all the way up to a new Land's End to John O'Groats of 2 days 22 hours 52 minutes and a 1,000 mile record of 3 days 11 hours 44 minutes. This was a largely unheralded and unrecognized athletic achievement; she was unfortunate that this ride was completed on 2 September 1939 and was rather overshadowed in the news. In addition women's cycling also appeared not infrequently in newsreels: Evelyn

Hamilton's achievement of 10,000 miles in 100 days (100 consecutive "century" rides) also made headlines in 1938. She was filmed numerous times by Pathé News as an example of athletic achievement and featured in film and at cycling exhibitions as a rider of Charles Mochet's velo-velocar and other recumbent cycles (even if film shots spent an inordinate time lingering on her ankles) (Cox, 2013).

Petronella's columns in the *Gazette* portrayed women as having the potential to be independent and self-reliant. Such qualities were not automatic but needed to be trained and nurtured: especially given the social forces with which they were contending. The strength of the social norms of marriage and responsibility for house holding and child rearing need not mean a retreat from public space. Instead, cycle technologies enabled a child to accompany its mother in her own social activities, through sidecar, child-seat, (Rann) trailer-bikes and finally into independent riding. Petronella was careful to extol the capabilities of girls' riding, for example, reporting a ten-year-old girl's first "century" ride (that is, a 100-mile distance. Peckham to Kings Lynn, 102 miles, *Gazette*, February 1939, p. 39) alongside her coverage of established professionals. The presentation of women cyclists as both heroic and capable role models is similar to the popular celebration of women's achievement in other mobility spheres at the time, for example, in the celebration of and widespread public fascination with Amy Johnson. It was easier for women to break through and define more equal roles in these new areas of activity than in areas of life where power and privilege were more firmly entrenched.

In sum, the situation for women in the 1930s cycling scene was of dramatic achievements in the UK and contains clear elements of role equality as an emancipatory process. The gains made in suffrage were being matched, at least in these lower-middle-class ranks, with changes in the expectations of social behaviours and obvious redefinitions of the public and private spheres, alongside changed considerations of parenting and domesticity. These gains were to prove short-lived.

The War and its Aftermath

As the bicycle became the primary household transport mode for many middle-class car-owning households in the face of petrol rationing, the war years saw a further boost to the numbers of utility riders. Additionally and, perhaps counter-intuitively, wartime also saw the beginning of massed-start cycle racing on British roads and the founding of a new rival organization to the NCU (see Cox 2016 for further analysis of post-war British cycling). In the CTC, women began to take a more visible role in organization and leadership (*Gazette*, May 1940, p. 116). But paper rationing reduced the journal to a minimum and Petronella's pages disappeared, along with most other regular columns. At the end of the war, "Wheelwisdom" was not reinstated. Its potential replacement, "Wheels and the Woman", penned by CTC Headquarters staff member Val Tomlinson, did not appear until April 1949 (p. 55). Tomlinson's initial comment questioned the lack of women as represent-atives in committees and decision-making bodies in the CTC. Despite providing some one-third of applicants for overseas tours, and a considerable proportion of local runs leadership, women, she complained, were largely invisible at the national level. "Wheels and the Woman" was short lived, lasting only a year, and only appearing as a bi-monthly article towards the back of the *Gazette*, rather than as a leading feature as "Wheel-wisdom" had been. Topics reverted to familiar issues, breaking no new ground. When considering clothing, emphasis was on the need for a tidy personal appearance, not the practical and pragmatic approach of Petronella. When reviewing the 1949 Cycle Show, Tomlinson argued the need for open frame versions of popular models: in order to allow for the possibility of riding in skirts. It appeared that the radicalism of ten years before was firmly dismissed, transformed by the flux and retrenchment in gender roles brought about by the aftermath of war.

After another gap without any specific women's advocacy, in August 1951 (*Gazette*, p. 411) seventeen-year-old Winifred Munday began what was to become an occasional feature under the title of a "Girl's Eye View". The degree of change in the broader outlook can be gauged by her observation that "there is something about a women's column [in the *Gazette*] that makes men laugh" (*Gazette*, October 1951, p. 361). Again, regardless of the numbers of women taking leading roles in CTC activities, gender roles had become considerably more ossified. "When writing your women's page, extol women riders for their grace and for their womanly contribution to the club, but keep at the back of your mind that cycling is fundamentally a man's game" wrote A. F. Searle (*Gazette*, April 1952, p. 570). Although a defence was given, Munday's response lacked the scorn of Petronella's stylish put-downs of male detractors. Responding to the accusation that women were not reliable long-term club members, leaving to start families, Munday's reply was muted: "A bird of passage she may be, but when her responsibilities as home-maker are over, she invariably returns – or at least makes it possible for her male partner to carry on" (p. 571). It was left to male correspondents in later months to point out that the majority of men also only ride for limited time periods and are equally unreliable long-term members.

Although Munday covered many of the same familiar topics in the five years of her writing in the *Gazette* (clothing, saddles, women riders), the reduction in the title of "Women" to "Girls" served only to marginalize and infantilize women's contributions. Increasingly, women's riding was associated only with family riding, the solo woman rider being almost entirely invisible. Women made their appearances only as an adjunct to men: this despite women like Val Tomlinson being a key CTC

Alpine tour leader throughout the 1950s (*Gazette*, November 1956, p. 328; February 1959, p. 47). The post-war situation of gender roles within the club had become radically transformed. Despite the emergence of a new generation of record-breaking women road riders such as Eileen Sheridan, and later Beryl Burton, there were few visible role models in the touring scene. The *Gazette* became an almost exclusively male preserve.

The barriers maintained by (mainly older) men in the club that Munday had complained about (*Gazette*, September 1952, p. 768) were firmly entrenched by the 1960s. The *Gazette*'s editorial in March 1961 (p. 55) places the dominant male understanding of women's place and role in cycle touring in perspective.

> 'The Ladies' has always been a favourite toast at club dinners, but during the past few months the proposers have, in many cases, spoken with a tinge of regret that there are not more of these charming companions to make the wonderful game of cycling more wonderful still.

Is it any wonder that women left and stayed away? The article went on to comment that women had never made up more than one-third of members (without noting the irony of this as an extremely high level of participation) and displayed its own inability to see women as other than wives or prospective wives, emphasizing that "our leading cyclists have consistently shown that they can look as attractive as any other sportswomen". Women had become no more than decorative.

Correspondence only served to reinforce these gender role stereotypes: "It is a waste of time to go out of one's way to cater for lady members ... we must face the fact that cycling does not appeal to women very much" (*Gazette*, March 1962, p. 58). The larger reality was that these comments were being made against a background of rapidly falling numbers of cycle users among the entire population and dramatic falls in club membership. Women appear to have become a scapegoat for broader changes.

In reality, however, women's cycling was in far less of a decline than men's during this period (Pooley et al., 2013, p.23)

Sexist comments and attitudes did not go unopposed. "If the CTC really wants more women members might I suggest that a less patronizing attitude on the part of the male cyclists would help", stated the headline letter in October 1963, singling out for particular attention the cartoonist "who usually shows the 'little woman' in a humorously derogatory way". Overall, however, such protestations were rather lost. The focus of the entire journal throughout the 1950s had been increasingly narrow and introspective, lacking in the broader focus and outward perspective of its pre-war editions. Women had become all but invisible in the *Gazette* as club membership dwindled to less than 8,000 (excluding the 5,000 or so life members). Cycle touring became an increasingly esoteric activity as other leisure possibilities expanded alongside increasing car ownership among the middle classes who had made up the core of the pre-war members. Yet among these die-hards, photographs indicate that women still made up typically one-third of CTC organized touring parties in the 1960s – just as they had always done (See *Cycletouring*, April/May 1978, p. 87).

A Minor Resurgence?
Re-launched in 1963 as *Cycletouring*, the club journal began to return to its pre-war style (though in a bi-monthly format). It deliberately presented a broad range of touring-related topics in order to give a broader appeal as more of a general interest magazine rather than the insiders' newsletter it had become. But radicalism and the sense of leadership visible in its earlier presentation of women was conspicuously absent. Not until 1973 – a decade after the revolution in unisex cycle design that the Moulton had initiated – did the issues of women's touring reappear. Major changes had occurred in British bicycle use in the 1960s, with mass sales of small-wheel bicycles marketed as style and fashion articles: an image powerful enough to have

halted, at least temporarily, a long-term decline in British cycle sales (Hadland, 2011). Apart from some generally sceptical reports (and interminable correspondence) on the merits or otherwise of small-wheeled bicycles, the changes in riding patterns from organized club activities to increasingly casualized leisure, almost entirely bypassed the CTC. Similarly the social changes in women's lives that also began in the 1960s were agonizingly slow to filter through, but in 1973, *Cycletouring* published its first acknowledgement that changes were awheel.

Anne Taylor wrote about her experience of women-only touring groups: "we abandoned our children (we prayed for them) to their fathers' care", she wrote, making light of the situation of organizing a women-only ride (*Cycletouring*, April/ May 1973, p. 81). The fact that the article needed to be headlined "Women's Lib" signalled just how unusual this perspective was in *Cycletouring*. Referring to the division of childcare to allow one parent a day of activity to themselves she wrote that, "In this enlightened age the time may well come when she is the one to cycle away". Thirty-five years previously, women's continued riding, even whilst caring for young children, was a normal and expected activity. The comments shows just how significant had been the degree of retrenchment in gender roles. The gendered identity of cycling even extended to children's riding. Bill Rann, who worked for both Holdsworth and Grubb cycle manu-facturers, developed the Trailerbike (one wheel with saddle and pedals attaching to the rear of the adult's machine) in the mid 1930s as an alternative to the childback tandem, the other frequent means to allow children to cycle with a parent. When Bill Hannington started to build trailerbikes in the late 1970s (as Hann trailers), he felt the need to produce them in both boys' and girls' versions (with and without top tubes) as opposed to the universal design of the original Rann. Even children's first forays into riding had now become clearly gendered.

Women and Cycling in Britain

It may be argued that the almost complete absence of specific consideration of women's cycle touring in the pages of the post-war CTC journals could be an indication of gender neutrality. However, in a situation of inequality, not to address difference is to perpetuate that inequality. Through the 1930s women's social roles and appropriate behaviours had been presented as malleable, open to negotiation and experimenttation. Domesticity was a fixed social obligation but cycling was presented as a means by which the isolation of householding could be overcome. The solidification of perceptions around women as non-cycle tourists, or as cycle touring only as accompanists of men and as guardians of children, is very much a post-war phenomenon. It needs reiterating that this analysis reflects the experiences of a strongly lower-middle-class organization, but oral testimony appears to bear out these findings from a wider group (Langhamer, 2000).

But during the 1970s, the changes in women's lives in wider society began to be reflected in organisational life. As the CTC approached its centenary year in 1978, the visibility of women in the pages of *Cycletouring* grew considerably and it reflected more of the reality of women's cycle touring. Overall numbers were now also increasing: up to 28,000 in 1975, approaching pre-war levels. For some, such as Molly Given (writing about solo touring in the West of Ireland, June/July 1978, pp. 130–132), the issue of gendered roles is not even worth a mention. Accounts are presented in *Cycletouring* of the personal reflections of touring and one cannot tell from the writing the sex of the journalist concerned. Many reports similarly reflect the experience of couples on tour together. For other women writing, the issue of lack of mechanical aptitude – even of basic practices such as mending a puncture – remained noteworthy. At grass roots and local level, women still made up significant portions of the backbone of the club's mundane riding activities. Although data is hard to come by, it appears that much of the local organizing fell to women in the individual sections. Cycle touring offered a social and leisure practice and a normal way of life, which may not be entirely unconnected with the gendered status of driving licence ownership during this period. Although 50% of households had access to a car at the beginning of the 1970s, driving was a predominantly male activity. The bicycle still offered the only real means of mobility for the majority of women. In the 1980s, a new image of women riding appeared, spurred on by the foundation of magazines such as *New Cyclist*. It reflected new thinking about the social and political role of the bicycle, but existed largely outwith the activities of the CTC.

Conclusions

The overview presented in this chapter opens up a number of avenues for further exploration. Questions can be asked around technologies and their affordances. The relationship of women's cycling to the presence (or absence) of particular technologies is complex. In the 1930s, women drove design innovation in order to create more appropriate technologies. In the 1960s, as cycles were increasingly marketed specifically at women, they re-created an image of the bicycle as a plaything. These tangled relationships continue to the present.

Women-only rides have become very significant in the past recent resurgence of organized cycling, not only in Britain. These are connected, as before, with the imagery of (and in the twenty-first century, actual support by) sporting celebrities. Once more, cycling magazines are filled with pages of discussion on appropriate clothing and presentation issues for women on bikes. On a more theoretical understanding we may consider the evidence produced above in terms of theories of social practice. Shove et al., (2012) identify practices as comprised of interacting elements of technologies, meanings and competences. We might use this example of women's cycle touring to explore how a single social practice of cycle touring has generated dramatically changing meanings and competences, relating to other forms of social roles and social practices. Above all, perhaps, the study demonstrates the complex and shifting identities produced and reproduced in women's cycling. Focusing on the cultural construction of these images, in the context of broader social roles, brings them into sharper focus.

Cycling was a signal of emancipation not only in the nineteenth century. Right up until the Second World War, it continued to provide a means of liberation and a way to redefine gender roles for British women. In the years when the enfranchisement of women was still recent news, the bicycle became a vehicle through which to express the newly emancipated state, as well as (as Eastman observed) having been one of the means by which the argument was made in the first place. In the post-war years, however, the assertion of cycle touring as a masculine activity appears to have restricted women's range of acceptable activity to narrower confines which would take many decades to be challenged. Cycle touring shifted to being one of the arenas in which hegemonic masculinities were performed (despite the reality of women's constant presence in touring as an activity). As women's riding re-emerged into visibility in the 1970s, it did so as a reflection of increasing emphasis on women's visibility in other spheres of life, not as a means to realizing that liberation.

References

Gazette and *Cycletouring* entries are given in text.

Bleckmann, D. (1998). *Wehe wenn sie losgelassen! Über die Anfänge des Frauenradfahrens in Deutschland.* Leipzig, Germany: Maxime.

Cox, P. (2012). "A Denial of Our Boasted Civilisation": Cyclists' Views on Conflicts over Road Use in Britain, 1926–1935, *Transfers*, 2(2), 4–30.

Cox, P. (2013). Human-Powered-Vehicles in Britain, 1930–1980. In A. Ritchie (ed.), *Proceedings of the 21st International Cycling History Conference, Prague, August 5th–7th, 2010*. London, UK: Cycling History (Publishing) Ltd.

Cox, P. (2016). Towards a Better Understanding of Bicycles as Transport. In C. Kopper & M. Moraglio (eds.). *The Organization of Transport: A History of Users, Industry, and Public Policy* (pp. 49–67). London, UK: Routledge.

Cox, P. (2015). Rethinking Bicycle Histories. In T. Männistö-Funk & T. Myllyntaus (eds.), *The Invisible Bicycle: New Insights into Bicycle History* (Technology and Change in History series). Leiden, Netherlands: Brill.

Cycling for Women: Eminent Medical Authorities Express Themselves in Plain Terms, *The Wheel & Cycle Trader*, 30 November 1894, 25.

Durham, M. (1998). *Women and Fascism*. Oxford, UK: Berg.

Eastman, C. (1978). *On Women and Revolution* [selections from her writings edited by Blanche Wiesen-Cook]. Oxford, UK: Oxford University Press.

Ebert, A.K. (2010). *Radelde Nationen: Die Geschicht des Fahrrads in Deutschland und den Nederlanden bis 1940*. Frankfurt, Germany: Campus Verlag.

Faulkner, W. (2001). The Technology Question in Feminism: A View from Feminist Technology Studies. *Women's Studies International Forum*, 24(1), 79–95.

Gardiner, J. (2010). *The Thirties: An Intimate History*. London, UK: Harper Collins.

Hadland, T. (2011). *Raleigh: Past and Presence of the Iconic Bicycle Brand*. London, UK: Cycle Publishing.

Herlihy, D.V. (2004). *The Bicycle*. New Haven, CT: Yale University Press.

Irwin, S. (2003). Interdependencies, Values and the Reshaping of Difference: Gender and Generation at the Birth of Twentieth-Century Modernity. *British Journal of Sociology,* 54(4), 565–584.

Johns, S.M. (2003). *Noblewomen, Aristocracy and Power in the Twelfth-Century Anglo-Norman Realm.* Manchester, UK: Manchester University Press.

Johnson, L., & Lloyd, J. (2004). *Sentenced to Everyday Life: Feminism and the Housewife.* Oxford, UK: Berg.

Langhamer, C. (2000). *Women's Leisure in England 1920–1960.* Manchester, UK: Manchester University Press.

McGurn, J. (1999). *On Your Bicycle: The Illustrated Story of Cycling* (new edition). York, UK: Open Road.

Nathan, Major. (1930). *Hansard* ref: ROAD TRAFFIC BILL [Lords] HC Deb, 18 February 1930, vol. 235, cc1203–343.

Norcliffe, G. (2001). *The Ride to Modernity: The Bicycle in Canada 1869–1900.* Toronto, Canada: University of Toronto Press.

Oddy, N. (1995). The Bicycle, an Exercise in Gendered Design. *Cycle History: Proceedings of the 5th International Cycling History Conference Cambridge, England, September 1994.* San Francisco, CA: Bicycle Books.

Pooley, C., Jones, T., Tight, M., Horton, D., Scheldeman, G., Jopson, A., & Strano, E. (2013). *Promoting Walking and Cycling: New Perspectives on Sustainable Travel.* Bristol, UK: Policy Press.

Pye, D. (1995). *Fellowship is Life: The Story of the Clarion Cycling Club.* Bolton, UK: Clarion Publishing.

Salleh, A. (1997). *Ecofeminism as Politics: Nature, Marx and the Postmodern.* London, UK: Zed Books.

Shove, E., Pantzar, M., & Watson, M. (2012). *The Dynamics of Social Practice: Everyday Life and How it Changes.* London, UK: Sage.

Strange, L.S., & Brown, R.S. (2002). The Bicycle, Women's Rights, and Elizabeth Cady Stanton. *Women's Studies, 31,* 609–626.

Welke, S., & Allen, J. (2004). Cycling Freedom for Women: Barriers for Women Cyclists Around the World. *Women and Environments International Magazine,* Spring/Summer, 34–36.

POSTSCRIPT

CYCLING CULTURES,
CULTURE AND CYCLING

Peter Cox

In his wide-reaching survey of current research into cycling, Harry Oosterhuis observes that a central research question frames much recent work: "why people use or don't use the bicycle for utilitarian purposes and, consequently, how cycling can be promoted" (2014, p. 20). The authors of this volume are unmistakably part of this trend, bridging academic and policy worlds, struggling on the edges between the (assumed) disinterested analysis of traditional academic perspectives and the active world of advocacy. Collectively, we acknowledge that we each have a standpoint, that in the search for more sustainable and more joyous ways of living we each would argue that the bicycle has a part to play, and one that is not currently fully realized. Of course, this is not to say that we all necessarily agree with each other or share more in our methods and approaches than this common underlying research question. The chapters presented here have emerged from and reflect a range of theoretical perspectives, analyses and experiences, and are part of a broader set of networks of studies which grows rapidly and spans across academic disciplines, as well as linking academia and practice.

Oosterhuis also concludes that in order to further this shared question, "Research into utilitarian cycling would benefit from a new approach that attends to national historical trajectories and national bicycle habitus" (Oosterhuis, 2014, p. 35). While the book overall presents a range of studies from different national locations, they are very much rooted in their own place specificity. And to take the Bourdieusian model further then we can see that the chapters assembled here, in their

203

different ways, work together to explicate different dimensions of habitus: not only the uses and practices of the bicycle, but also the elements of doxa – the accepted beliefs and attitudes – that inform actions and conceptualizations of cycling. To accomplish this, we will also need to cast our gaze beyond the specifics of utilitarian cycling to understand cycling practices that are unconnected to utilitarian uses, and to other cultural processes and practices that shape public understanding of cycling, as the chapters in this volume attest.

The task of this final section is to continue the dialogues opened by the individual contributions in light of the overall concern of the volume, to revisit the chapters and consider how they speak to each other and to the questions raised at the opening of the book. Firstly, it revisits the idea of culture set out in Chapter 1, considering how our understandings of culture help us to read the individual contributions. Secondly, attention will briefly be drawn to each chapter in turn to show how they speak to each other, as well as to elucidate some themes that emerge from the whole project. Thus we also may be able to provide insight into the way in which such very different subject matters as are covered here contribute to the formation of a broader multifaceted narrative. It is a narrative that thinks about cycling not simply as a physical activity, or even as a diverse set of practices, but as a cultural activity, one that forms part of twentieth-century European history, with both a past and future. Cycling is part of culture, not just a culture in its own right.

Across the whole span of the book, we can see three recurrent dimensions of culture. First and perhaps most obviously we can talk about culture as summary behaviour. Particular groups of users forge their own identities and styles. For example, in Bunte's study (Chapter 7) we are offered an insight into the world of German long-distance randonneurs and shown that it is not only their own self-definition that matters. Unpicking the strands of their practices shows us not only the contrasts and parallels to other forms of participant cycle sport, but also the high degree of continuity with some of the practices of cycle tourists in the 1930s (Chapter 8).

These images of culture as the collective experiences of particular groups, encourage an almost anthropological gaze, examining the practices of a range of different groups and describing the worlds they inhabit. We might read the identities of cargo bike users (Chapter 6) in the same manner. In the 1890s and early 1900s they signified modernity, a source of pride and celebration as shown in the spectacular Parisian races. When cargo bikes were mundane tools of the retail trade, to be a rider of such machines was of little import. By the late 1950s they were marginalized and the rider a figure of fun. Only when they started being renovated and produced by and among user groups (subsequently spreading to wider markets) did they become a badge of identity – a source of proudly independent status and signifiers of challenge to the values and practices of car-dominated societies. Today's commercial use has to negotiate carefully between these competing images to re-establish itself as the mark of an efficient logistics net.

Whether cycling is marginal or mainstream, it is clear that while we may identify specific sets of practices of cycling with their associated, styles and images, and that these can usefully be analysed in terms of subcultures, homogenization into singular identities, even within these subgroups, is both inac-curate and potentially problematic. Revisiting Shove et al.'s (2012) examination of practices as interactions of competences, meanings and materials (discussed in Chapter 1) assists our interpretations of the activities of subcultures in their formation and in their changing identities over time. Importantly, we can note that practices are not entirely self-determined. The importance of external factors, how meaning is imputed to actions by outside observers, is a vital element of this. Women's cycle touring (Chapter 8) was redefined in the 1950s, not by its practitioners, who carried on their activities much as they had done previously, but because of the changing external realities of gender roles in post-war Britain. The maternalist dimensions of policies (particularly those concerned with welfare) framed around expectations that a woman's place is in the home, assisted a changing climate of expectation around what was appropriate, or even possible, for women (Fielding, 2003).

This brings us to the second dimension of culture: that of context. Meanings are not imputed to practices simply through acts of will or as products of inevitable circumstances, but within the context of wider social structures, political regimes and physical spaces. The political and social dimensions are explicated clearly by Horton and Jones' (Chapter 3), and also form the basis of much of Sabelis' discussion (Chapter 2). But to take the latter of those dimensions, we might ask about the specific contexts in which cycling is taking place. Physical spaces can be made hostile or welcoming. Hostility or welcome are not only produced by physical properties but are also produced by signals and in symbolic form. The mapping of spaces is highlighted by Deegan (Chapter 5) demonstrates that exactly the same space can be conceptualized and communicated in different ways. If a map is a narrative of a space, we need constantly to think about the stories we tell, who are they about? How do the subjects of the stories relate to the world around them? Are they strangers to it, needing survival skills to be taught or does a map provide a guide to one's citizenship? Context also frames the implicit dialogue between Chapters (2, 3, and 4) that between them provide the contrast between the current Dutch and English situations. Divergent policy trajectories over a long time period frame everyday cycling in radically different ways. Place still matters in the human-experience oriented world of spatial mobility by bicycle.

Postscript

The final dimension of culture is the ideological, contained not just by the political discourses which deal with the subject directly, but the broader signifying practices within society. Which dimensions of activity are seen as important, which held up as desirable and which denigrated? Which groups of people are deemed to matter, to be worth investing in? Although at one level these disparate studies deal with a broad range of topics, this ideological dimension runs throughout. Subcultures make ideological comment (explicit or not) on the broader contexts in which they operate. Dominant cultures express ideological convictions of their own in order to maintain their dominance. Although the impact of political ideology is most strikingly illustrated by Horton and Jones (Chapter 3) and in the withdrawal of funding for the programmes in van der Kloof's work (Chapter 4), we can see a thread in all of the chapters.

A Kaleidoscopic View

Although writing from a variety of viewpoints, of professional identities and from differing national and regional contexts, the authors here connect through a shared commitment to change. During the meetings that led to this volume, the metaphor of the kaleidoscope was used to describe our view of cycling. Different fragments falling into place are constantly rearranged and the viewer sees how the shifting shapes make patterns. Individual elements overlap and interrelate, and this final section will demonstrate some of the patterns formed out of the interrelations of the different parts of the book.

By focusing on the perceptions of a relatively marginal group within a context where cycling is generally regarded as a mainstream and relatively unremarkable form of travel, Sabelis (Chapter 2) raises the question of how to manage diversity to the benefit of all. She reveals the variety of cycling practices, even within the context of transport and utility cycling in the Netherlands, as complex and politically laden. This complexity is not just a matter of observed diversity of riding speeds and machinery, but of how elements interact in the cycling spaces provided. And in order to comprehend these spaces, one needs to examine the political contexts in which policy is formed. While the Netherlands may have a reputation as a cycle-friendly nation, we can see how local policy is crucial. If we combine these insights with those in van der Kloof's study we can see how this singular image of cycling in the Netherlands conceals a multiplicity of practices and is distinguished not just by the type of riding (Sabelis) but also by age and gender and further by place of origin. Geographic and demographic factors interplay with economic ones to shape cycling practices, and political priorities can be used to both enable and hinder participation rates. The ability of cycling policies to disappear between election manifestos and programmes of action, even where there is a general consensus on the importance of cycling, is also a salutary lesson for those engaged in processes of change.

Sabelis' observation is that the needs of a smaller group, necessarily enthusiasts for their cycling and, those who have made deliberate choices to travel differently from the norms of a generally bicycle-positive culture, can have useful lessons for wider inclusivity. But for Horton and Jones (Chapter 3), the attitudes and practices of the cyclist by choice in Britain, are not necessarily the best guide to assess what is needed to open up opportunities to change transport practices. The context is again vitally important. Sabelis' comments are made in a context where fear and insecurity are not significant barriers for the majority. Where they are, in van der Kloof's experience, these fears can be dealt with in an individual context. Her trainees are being sent out into situations where everyday journeys are expected to be made by bike – they are joining in and blending in with the routine everyday practices that see them better integrated into mundane urban life. Objectively, cycling may not be as dangerous in the UK as it is often portrayed, but the reality is that the environment of cycling in most cities is hostile, as Horton and Jones vividly point out. Training people to ride in most of England prepares them to be part of a highly visible minority. Relating this back to social practice theory, the structural contexts and material spaces of the UK and the Netherlands impute very different meanings to practices of quotidian cycling, and the competences required within those structures are also quite different. A further observation that must be reiterated from these three papers is the degree to which all highlight the variety and multiplicity of peoples, practices and understandings that can be hidden behind a simple description of utility cycling.

As well as van der Kloof's presentation of the detailed statistics on cycle use which reveal unfolding stories of social group differentiation, her analysis of the gendered and classed nature of cycling connects with Cox's (Chapter 8) discussion of gender and cycling among British cycle tourists. Here one of the pertinent observations is that emancipatory gains made in any particular circumstance are not guaranteed to continue. The liberation provided by the bicycle to the generation of the 1930s was not sustained. Indeed, subsequent discourses around cycling reproduced and reinforced the limitation of gender roles enacted in broader social culture. Though some of the achievements and redefinition of women's roles among these cyclo-tourists are deeply progressive, we must also note that these gains were largely focused on a middle-class group of women who were relatively privileged and already beneficiaries from increased educational and social opportunities.

Among Petronella's suggestions (see Chapter 8) for getting a better understanding of where you live and more confidence in your travel by bike, was to take a map and colour in every road after you have ridden it. Deegan's (Chapter 5) consideration of cycle maps and mapping combines thinking about the internalized wayfinding skills that regular riders use in order to navigate, with the politics of (re)presentation inherent in the production of cycling maps. Which routes riders are directed towards creates a narrative of the expected behaviour of the rider, but it also indicates the relation of the mapmaker to the rider. Coding maps to show where there are segregated infrastructure routes, for example, is an immediate indication that route provision is not comprehensive. In the Netherlands and Dutch speaking areas of Belgium, a nodal point system is used on cycling guides, where only junctions are numbered, suggesting that every route connecting these numbered junctions is a suitable space to ride. Connecting Deegan's analysis to Horton and Jones' call for more radical rethinking, perhaps one might suggest that, more than providing maps to show where it is thought appropriate for cyclists to go, the injunction could be reversed. Motoring maps might perhaps more strongly show roads along which not to drive unless absolutely necessary, on the lines of the German Fahrradstrasse. The motoring map would become a specialist map, rather than the cycling map, as a subset of general road mapping. A strong ideological statement, perhaps, but in keeping with the radical suggestions made previously concerning the reversal of current cultural norms.

Extending our gaze beyond the utilitarian, Chapters 7 and 8 both explore the worlds of those who deliberately cycle for pleasure. That Bunte's randonneurs (Chapter 7) choose to push themselves to the limits of endurance may not immediately resonate with the usual descriptions of pleasure (except in a peculiarly masochistic way). Their actions are nevertheless chosen, and the mobilization of personal resources for training and preparation are common to most amateur sporting endeavours when undertaken seriously: one only has to consider the thousands who train for and participate in marathon running to see this level of dedication elsewhere. Studies of cycling for sport and leisure are not frequently included in discussions dominated by an underlying concern for utilitarian cycling, but their inclusion here reflects both the breadth of cycling cultures and the necessity for comprehending the diversity of practices in a cultural approach to the problems of cycling policy.

While cycling for transport remains negligible in the UK, there has been a marked growth in recreational and sporting cycling, associated with some changes in the public images of cycling. But there remains a tension between the imagery of sport cycling as an activity beyond the capacity of most people (as Bunte shows) that hinders its integration and connection with more mundane cycling practices. The emphasis on making riding of any kind pleasurable, so clearly visible in the 1930s CTC writing on women and cycling (Chapter 8), is one way in which these worlds can be integrated. Properly designed, comprehensive networks of segregated paths clearly ensure that travelling by bike is an attractive option, as the bigger research project in which Horton and Jones participated concluded (Pooley et al., 2013).

The importance of good design in order to include, not exclude, was the starting point for Sabelis' study. One particular core test, which had only just begun to be identified even in the Dutch CROW *Design Manual for Bicycle Traffic* (CROW, 2007) is the usability of facilities by non-standard cycles. Although individual European nations may have their own specific regulations on maximum widths for tricycles, Velomobiles and cargo bikes, especially when carrying loads, will demonstrate whether built infrastructure is inclusive or exclusive. Cox and Rzewnicki's study (Chapter 6) of cargo bikes illustrates how not just bicycle riding but also cycle technologies are tied into society. As proponents of the study of the social construction of technology (SCOT) have long argued, cycles are not simply objects to be interpreted in isolation, but constitute socio-technical systems (Bijker, 1995). All the chapters identify space as an important element either as a technology in itself or as the dimension in which technologies are deployed: whether physically in infrastructure or conceptually as mapping. The integration of cargo bikes into the spaces of cycling, and the challenges they may pose for current assumptions about infrastructure (for example, turning circles or parking spaces) are important elements in planning for sustainable transport futures. Again here we can cross reference Sabelis' (Chapter 2) principle of coping with diversity through inclusivity. Given the degree to which diversity is an integral assumption of many European strategies for increased cycling shares of traffic, we should only expect the growth of cargo bike use to continue.

Multiplicity, Diversity and Complexity

Recognition of multiplicity, diversity and complexity as characteristic of cycling, not just today but historically, and not just in those areas where cycling is a major form of transport or everyday activity, poses questions for Oosterhuis' underlying question cited at the beginning of this chapter. What exactly is being promoted? How can we cope with pluralism and how can the social divisions of ethnicity, class, age and impairment be incorporated into the advocacy process? Our volume cannot hope to respond to all these, neither is its task to do so. But by raising these issues, and exploring some areas and ways of thinking that we consider may be important contributory factors in the addressing of these problems, we begin to assist this process.

Recalling again the image of the kaleidoscope, each image seen is formed from the juxtaposition of selected elements. As individual pieces move around, new patterns emerge. No single volume could hope to provide a comprehensive analysis of cycling cultures nor a complete cultural analysis of cycling in its myriad forms. However, through the presentation of these studies and their juxtaposition within a shared framework we see them in different ways. Similarly, the places and the roles of

212

cycling appear differently as we approach their variety from a range of perspectives.

In linear patterns of thought, diversity and multiplicity become problems, not fitting easily within the frameworks of direct cause and effect: problem analysis, intervention and measurable outcome. Comprehending the issues of sustainability and mobility as forms of complexity, however, puts a different perspective on things (Urry, 2007). A kaleidoscope is a chaotic system. There is not simple predictability as to how the elements will fall and what sort of a pattern will emerge. Complex problems are not generally amenable to linear solutions, but that does not make them insoluble. Understanding the problems as complex, however, means that the diversity of actions and practices, the multiplicity of ways of looking at them and the worlds of activity with which cycling is connected, are not a hindrance but a necessary part of the solution.

If what we are looking for is as Horton and Jones put it, a plural mobility, then we can perhaps return to the arguments made in Chapter 1. The study of cycling cultures, revealing their complexity, diversity and often contradictory realities and experiences, allows us to discover their interdependencies. The context in which all the authors of the volume met was that of a broad-based advocacy movement, working for changes to the currently unsustainable – socially and environmentally – patterns of European transport. It has been their differences of outlook and experience that have necessitated consideration of how solidarity is built, not through identification of that which is the same, but across the divides of geography and cultures. Cycling cultures are not simple, unitary identities of uniform groups, but thinking about cycling in terms of culture allows us to better comprehend the implications for policy and practice in moving towards plural mobilities.

References

Bijker, W.E. (1995). *Of Bicycles, Bakelite and Bulbs: Toward a Theory of Socio-Technical Change.* Cambridge, MA: MIT Press.

CROW. (2007). *Design Manual for Bicycle Traffic* [English version]. Ede, Netherlands: CROW.

Fielding, S. (2003). *Labour and Cultural Change.* Manchester, UK: Manchester University Press.

Oosterhuis, H. (2014). Bicycle Research Between Bicycle Policies and Bicycle Culture. *Mobility in History, 5,* 20–36.

Pooley, C., Jones, T., Tight, M., Horton, D., Scheldeman, G., A. Jopson & E. Strano (2013). *Promoting Walking and Cycling: New Perspectives on Sustainable Travel.* Bristol, UK: Policy Press.

Shove, E., Pantzar, M., & Watson, M. (2012). *The Dynamics of Social Practice: Everyday Life and How it Changes.* London, UK: Sage.

Urry, J. (2007). *Mobilities.* Cambridge, UK: Polity Press.